Masking the Abject

Masking the Abject

A Genealogy of Play

Mechthild Nagel

LEXINGTON BOOKS
Lanham • Boulder • New York • Oxford

LEXINGTON BOOKS

Published in the United States of America
by Lexington Books
4720 Boston Way, Lanham, Maryland 20706

12 Hid's Copse Road
Cumnor Hill, Oxford OX2 9JJ, England

British Library Cataloguing in Publication Information Available

Library of Congress Cataloging-in-Publication Data

Nagel, Mechthild.
   Masking the abject : a genealogy of play / Mechthild Nagel.
     p. cm.
   Includes bibliographical references (p.) and index.
   ISBN 0-7391-0307-5 (alk. paper)—ISBN 0-7391-0308-3 (pbk. : alk. paper)
    1. Play (Philosophy) 2. Plato. 3. Aristotle. 4. Hegel, Georg Wilhelm Friedrich,
1770–1831. I. Title.

  B105.P54 N34 2001
  128'.4—dc21

                     2001049211

Printed in the United States of America

♾™ The paper used in this publication meets the minimum requirements of American
National Standard for Information Sciences—Permanence of Paper for Printed Library
Materials, ANSI/NISO Z39.48–1992.

For my parents,
Irene Nagel, née Argyropoulos, and Hans Nagel

Contents

Acknowledgments

A book on play has a peculiar self-referential status. A playful composure breaks down at multiple points throughout the writing process, fatigue sets in, and the spirit of gravity takes over. Perhaps another tract needs to be written to chronicle such failures of tossing masks and mocking oneself throughout. "Why I write so unplayfully about play" may have to be a recasting of the drama of writing and publishing. A number of people took interest in this project from the very beginning. I wish to thank my teachers Gareth Matthews, Ann Ferguson, and John Brentlinger for their support and tremendous encouragement for a thesis on play which eventually gave rise to this book. I am very grateful to Alison Brown, Angela Curran, Dion Farquhar, Marcella Tarozzi Goldsmith, Margaret Nash, and Bob Stone for sharing their insightful comments on the various stages of the manuscript. Andrew Cutrofello and Bill Martin read the entire manuscript and provided invaluable feedback and support. Special thanks to Professor Rainer Marten of Albert-Ludwigs Universität, Freiburg for a careful reading of the manuscript while he was recovering from an eye operation. Professor Marten inspired me to pursue philosophy with his Vorlesung "Ontologie als Ideologie" in 1985. His influence on my thinking perhaps seems smaller in this book than it truly is. Other Freiburg friends, especially Guido Löhrer, convinced me that it was possible to write a scholarly work on nonserious matters. Susan Buechler and Mark Thomas engaged in spirited discussions on the topic and helped cheerfully with endless formatting problems. I am also grateful to Tiyo Attallah Salah-El, Gino Bush, Ayca Cubukcu, Balam Kenter, and Michael Nieto García for their friendship and support. My families, both in the States and in Germany, were perhaps at times incredulous about this project, but the topic lends itself to much laughter and comic relief. I wish to thank Loni and David Saunders and my parents Irene and Hans Nagel for their unfailing financial and emotional support. Elisabeth, Rosi, Rolf, Irmgard, and Margarethe—thank you for teaching me how to play! I am also blessed with wonderful colleagues who enjoy playing and discussing social justice, Larry Ashley, Bernard Jackson, and Kathryn Russell.

Introduction

"And we say that serious things [*spoudaia*] are better than laughable things and those connected with amusement [*paidia*]."[1] With this innocuous statement Aristotle initiates the malediction of play in Western thought. Pursuit of playful matters in thought and ethical action becomes ideologically suspect in the eyes of the "we." Who is laughing, though? Playful enactments occupy the role of the "abject"[2]: Agitating in this process of abjection, we encounter "serious" thinkers who denounce play as an unworthy, childish, irrational, superficial activity, yet, curiously, philosophers are fascinated by it. What is repulsive draws us in further: we can't quite stand it, averting our eyes—in fact we tend to squint and pay even closer attention to the abjectionable stuff. In addition, perhaps there is an anxiety that the gods might laugh back at the good person who takes himself too seriously. To deride play becomes a sport, a race for legitimation: emphatically he claims that philosophy is not a game, not a trivial matter, which can be pursued by women or children or nonpropertied men (i.e., the masses or subaltern subjects).

In this study of Western play discourses normative questions are addressed, such as *what* gets excluded and *who* is not allowed to play. It is an exercise of ideological critique insofar as it attempts to highlight hidden agendas and the dis-ease of philosophers discussing what they prejudge as objectionable or suspect subjects.

Play is an elusive term which defies all conceptualization, in part because we are already so familiar with it. One way of describing it is by employing Wittgenstein's concept of family resemblance in order to avoid an idealization of a certain type of play to be favored over other suspect ones.[3] While this is an appealing description, it seems to me that it is not the appropriate tool to use in an ideology critique of philosophical encounters with play.

In focusing on the precarious ontological status of play, where play finds itself cast in opposition to seriousness, I am not talking about (many) games, sport, cultural activities—unless such actors elucidate something or, alternatively, hide behind masquerades (e.g., in the works of classic Greek dramaturgists, such as tragedy, comedy, epos). In reflecting play back onto the contemplative person, one needs to bring attention to the notion of a playful attitude exhibited by thinkers while they leisurely philosophize about the good life and first principles. In this context it is pertinent to look at play as power from Marxist and feminist motivated perspectives in order to differentiate between agonistic, violence-inciting ways of playing and cooperative, non-competitive ways of engaging playfully with others. Yet, it is difficult to maintain such a neat conceptual distinction, especially in the case of Socrates, who chooses combatativeness when engaging with sophist foes and dons a more caring tone when engaging with his equals or adolescent interlocutors.

Playfulness as a particular aesthetic attitude of the self also has ethical importance for the Greeks. After all, Aristotle's *eudaimonia* (happiness) is an end in itself, the ultimate telos of the human condition. Only a philosopher is properly predisposed to play; he enjoys proper seriousness and disdain for decadence and amusement. A certain leisurely attitude is needed to engage in *theoria*. Poets and philosophers alike ponder about the play of the divine and the human in the ancient world. In the Hellenic epoch the play of the satyr (masking the ludic[4] god Dionysus) dominates; gods play mockingly with the human fate of heroic warriors. And yet, playfulness also is the most divine attribute in humans, as Plato remarks cryptically in the *Laws*. What seems to be a comic chance-play in the gods is truly tragic in human ethical life because such play, or being toyed with by the divine puppeteers, is a gambling between life and death.

Where the Greek organic worldview emphasizes the *ethical* component in play (or leisure), the modern view, marked by possessive individualism, highlights the *aesthetic* aspect. No ancient thinker deems it necessary to give a logos of play (say, distinct from giving an account for mimesis. In modernity, by contrast, we see the beginning of a (master) theory of play. The industrial revolution and the ensuing embourgoisement of life change the focus from play versus seriousness (in ethical comportment) towards play versus work. How does the burgher spend his pastimes? Within philosophical discourse (since Baumgarten and Wolff), aesthetics is established as a separate region or sphere from epistemology and ethics.

Aesthetics deals with creative and free play outside the confines of physical or moral necessities. Leisurely play occurs for its own sake or for relaxation. (*L'art pour l'art!*) The modern worldview, especially that of Kant and Schiller, invokes the individualist play of the self, the self-grounding play of the imagination. The artist, the genius, creates the aesthetic standard and refuses to simply obey and reinterpret traditional standards. Principles such as creativity, freedom, and autonomy preoccupy the Enlightenment player whereas these concepts are certainly alien to the Aristotelian organic worldview.

Despite these ideological and ideosyncratic differences between the two epochs, we can identify one guiding thread, which is the interplay of Apollonian (logocentric) and Dionysian (tragic, Bacchanalian) forces. I rely on Nietzsche's terminology (from *Birth of Tragedy*), because these notions seem to best describe the ethical and aesthetic dimensions of play. These play impulses are not merely in binary opposition; rather, they should be thought of as being intertwined dialectically in a unity of opposites. The Apollonian principle, as the *principium individuationis*, makes the Dionysian bearable for us.[5]

In addition to using these Nietzschean principles, I interrogate the prevailing "jargon of authenticity" in play theories: whose game is favored or maligned? should one favor the adult's play over the child's play? does the genius, the artist have a special status? Johan Huizinga, famously, sets up rules for what counts as good life and good play in his study *Homo Ludens*.[6] For Huizinga, who follows the logic of authenticity, certain forms of play have to be rejected (such as professional sports, playing for money, for material benefits).[7] Thus in play theories which are under Aristotle's spell, Apollonian play wins out over Dionysian play.

I develop a genealogy of play within Western philosophy and analyze how play has come to be the Other of reason. Methodologically speaking, this study employs Nietzsche's analytic concepts with his own tools, yet it also attempts to go beyond Nietzsche. I draw on Nietzsche's oppositional pair of the Apollonian and Dionysian in characterizing play in ancient Greek and modern German thought. My main thesis is that one can trace a malediction of play to Aristotle, not Plato. This should lead to a reevaluation of Plato's philosophy (aesthetic theory) as "logocentric." Countering Nietzsche, I would like to suggest that the tragic, Dionysian play becomes eclipsed by Aristotle, not by Plato.

I am interested in studying the effects of the shift from a play-affirming perspective to a disapproving ethical attitude towards play. Much has been written about this shift, but mostly with respect to Plato's introduction of art as mimesis and Socrates' critique of Hellenic tragedy. In light of this shift of emphasis it has been argued—by Nietzsche in particular—that Socratic (Apollonian) irony and rationality triumph over a Heraclitean (Dionysian, tragic) notion of play. Many play theoreticians (e.g., Fink 1960; Heidemann 1968; Kutzner 1973; and Spariosu 1989) simply follow the lead of Nietzsche's attack on Socrates, displayed in *The Birth of Tragedy*. With this work Nietzsche initiates the *Mimesisstreit*, the persisting controversy which has ramifications for play theory with respect to Plato and Socrates' Apollonian attitudes towards mimesis and *paidia* (play). Following Nietzsche, Eugen Fink holds that play and (poetic) mimesis are contiguous concepts, and that in his harsh critique of the poets Plato succeeds in demystifying (*entzaubern*) play, relegating play to a lesser ontological status of "mere" play, that is, a play which is not serious. However, as classical philologists have noted, this ludic (i.e., playful) shift of positing the oppositional pair of play/seriousness predates Plato; in Herodotus's writings, for example, there are many references to play as being unreal (a mere jest), harmless (a mere child's play), and a relaxing activity. Play is thus contrasted with *spoude* (seriousness), which characterizes the serious activity of the adult.[8]

The structure of the book is as follows: In the first chapter we will look at conceptions of play ranging from Homer to Aristophanes. Several play theoreticians following Derrida and Heidegger have systematized play/power discourses of the Greeks using the categories of ancient proto-logo-rationality and classic/Attic rationality.[9] Spariosu (1991) differentiates between archaic/agonistic play and classic/median play where Hesiod serves as a nodal figure with his fable on the hawk and nightingale. Furthermore, he argues that in Hesiod's writings competitive values are displaced by a rational, cooperative fair play, which no longer glamorizes the warrior class. In this critique (of the Homeric world), what is conjured up are images of wild, out of control heroes (and gods) who play senselessly like untamed young innocent children; "might makes right" is the rule of the game. This interpretation seems plausible, but I have tried to give a more ambivalent, less oppositional reading of the Homeric epic. Also, I have trouble conceptualizing the Presocratic thought as proto- or prerational; to think of Homer, Hesiod, or Heraclitus as operating outside the strictures of the logos is a problematic romanticization.

The second chapter presents perhaps an affront to Nietzschean and post-Nietzschean sensibilities. Plato, who is thought of as the philosopher breaking with (tragic) play, is actually served up as a protagonist against Aristotle. Of course, this is a controversial claim, since Plato ranks mimesis (the art of the poets) as three times removed from the truth. Also mimesis is demoted to the status of "mere play" (*paidia tinas*) and not to be taken seriously. However, for Plato, in the right moment (*kairos*) play and seriousness are contiguous, exemplified in Agathon's eros-speech in the *Symposium*. In this dialogue a satyric Socrates stands in for Dionysus, toying with myths and masks while raising serious arguments about the nature of love.

In the third chapter, I will explore Aristotle's strategy to eclipse the Dionysian impulse: Play (*paidia*) becomes the Other (of reason) and only leisure (*schole*) is valuable for philosophical contemplation. *Paidia* is condemned in his ethics and utilized in the *Politics*. Thus Aristotle stresses the instrumental value of *paidia* for male children's and young men's education. Aristotle's peculiar malediction of play serves as a thread, a guideline for explicating the Apollonian tenor in modern play theory.

The fourth chapter discusses how both Kant and Schiller return to an Aristotelian validation of the Apollonian; they abandon this path in their conception of the aesthetic-anthropological perspectives of *Spiel*, where play is not cast as inferior to leisure. Yet, Kant unequivocally states that play lacks epistemological value and Schiller asserts a preference for the transcendental play-drive over a materialist one. Given this hierarchy, female subjectivities and other subaltern subjects seem to drop out of the play discourse.

Where Kant and Schiller are perhaps best characterized as transitional figures, in the last chapter, I argue that Hegel's *Phenomenology of Spirit* anticipates Nietzsche's "ludic turn." Hegel gives equal importance to the Dionysian and Apollonian play impulses. Rationalistic (Apollonian) dichotomies get deconstructed. Hegel compares Truth with a "Bacchanalian whirl" which is the interplay of drunken frenzy and calm repose. I argue that this metaphor of the revel is clearly Heraclitean in origin and I take the trope to be a central category for the interpretation of Hegel's account of play. Hence, I will argue against Deleuze, who narrowly views Hegel's dialectic as carrying a notion of *ressentiment* and a "spirit of gravity."

After Hegel, play discourses begin to proliferate; we see a discussion of play and developments of play theory in both left and right Hegelian tendencies. For this reason, this study will conclude with a chapter on Hegel, not Nietzsche nor contemporary play theorists; however, their perspectives inform my ideology critique. Nietzsche is the first play theorist to expose play as the Other of philosophical discourse, and he proceeds to affirm the Dionysian (frenzied, irrational) aspects of play (cf. *Zarathustra*, *Gay Science*). I argue that the so-called artist metaphysicians (Nietzsche, Deleuze, Fink, Gadamer) contribute to a paradigm shift, but, as heirs to the Enlightenment project, they do not explore sufficiently the subjectivities of players who have been placed as outsiders to Western metaphysics.

What significance, if any, does a historical reevaluation of play have for the philosophical enterprise? As a (postmodern) gesture against Enlightenment ideals, play (qua free play) has been used to conjure up the death of man (death of the monological, self-grounding subject). Playing with signifiers opens up the rigid horizon of logocentrism; the hermeneutic and poststructuralist play with ambiguities resist the semiotic confinement of grand theories. Yet, this waging war on totality has been fought on an agonistic playground. Is there another way of imagining a compassionate, sincere, violence-free playfulness which, at the same time, does not engage in a repression of difference? Recent contributions to ethical perspectives (care of the self, maternal care, lesbian ethics) all seem preoccupied with subduing the agonistic side—yet do they also leave the trickster perspectives, the queer desires behind? This book will not attempt to answer these questions but will perhaps serve as a provisional jumping board from which to begin to explore such important matters.

Notes

1. Aristotle, *Nicomachean Ethics*, 1177a.
2. This term is borrowed from Kristeva, *Powers of Horror: An Essay on Abjection* (New York: Columbia University Press, 1982).
3. "There is the tendency to look for something in common to all the entities which we commonly subsume under a general term. We are inclined to think that there must be something in common to all games, say, and that this common property is the justification for applying the general term 'game' to the various games; whereas games form a family the members of which have family likenesses" (Wittgenstein, *The Blue and Brown Books*. Oxford: Blackwell, 1975), 17.
4. "Ludic" is used descriptively as a technical term for "playful," but it specifically circumscribes the Dionysian trickster aspects of play.
5. On this point see Robert Ackermann, *Nietzsche: A Frenzied Look* (Amherst: University of Massachusetts Press, 1990). For a feminist reading of these aesthetic principles, see Caroline Picart, *Resentment and the "Feminine" in Nietzsche's Politico-Aesthetics*, (University Park, Pa.: Penn State University Press, 1999).
6. See Huizinga's seminal book *Homo Ludens* (Boston: Beacon Press, 1950).
7. For a critique of Huizinga's conception of play, see my article "Play in Culture and the Jargon of Primordiality: A Critique of Huizinga's *Homo Ludens*," in *Play and Culture Studies*, vol. 1 (Duncan et al., ed. Greenwich, Conn.: Ablex Publications, 1998).
8. On this point, see Hermann Gundert, "Zum Spiel bei Platon," in *Beispiele. Festschrift für Eugen Fink zum 60. Geburtstag* (Den Haag: Nijhoff, 1965), 190.
9. I am thinking here particularly of Mihai Spariosu's book, *God of Many Names: Play, Poetry, and Power in Hellenic Thought from Homer to Aristotle* (Durham, N.C.: Duke University, 1991).

Chapter 1

TRAGIC PLAY IN THE PRESOCRATIC WORLD

Es ist ein Spiel, nehmt's nicht zu pathetisch, und vor Allem nicht moralisch!
—Friedrich Nietzsche, *Philosophie im tragischen Zeitalter der Griechen*

Mapping out a philosophical conception of play among the Presocratic thinkers requires a certain disposition, perhaps a desire to "go native" or, in this case "to go Greek." In their attempt of uncovering the origins of the logos of play in Western metaphysics, philosophers have gone to great lengths to eschew their modernist (or late modernist) prejudices in order to chart the ancient terrain with greater purity. Yet, unwittingly those values tend to be reinscribed into their discourses. Thus, Nietzsche's break with his contemporaries' philistine world-view is only partially successful, when he uses the notion of innocence to describe the playful attitude of the Greek boy child in Homer's *Iliad*. In a presentist move, Nietzsche takes the language of contemporary child psychology and inscribes it onto the Homeric world. This is only one of many examples why the quest for purity or authenticity is always already doomed. In Nietzsche's case, it is the desire to find an epoch where playful discourse has not yet been contaminated with the logocentrism of Socrates. The greater the urge to weed out impurities, the more persistent they tend to stick to the master narrative.

What kind of play characterizes the ancient Hellenic texts? In a broad sense, play tends to be an autotelic activity, in other words, an activity the Hellenic nobles engage in for its own sake; at the same time play may be an act which is worthless in a functional sense and characterized as futile, nonserious, unproductive, ignorant, and childish. But there are exceptions to this definition. Odysseus's bags of tricks include playing games with his opponents to seek strategic advantage.

In the archaic and classical Hellenic periods, there is no single Greek word which covers all aspects of the English term "play" (as in playing games, dramatic play, play as opposed to work, etc.). Besides the obvious terms such as *paidia* and *paignion* we have to consider other words as well (e.g., *agon, athlos, eris, tuche, ananke, charme, schole, diagoge, paideia, mimesis*).[1] We can however observe a shift in emphasis. Whereas *paidia*, i.e., child's play, is absent in Homer, it gains prominence in the works of the fifth and fourth centuries.[2] In interpreting the semantic shifts of play in Homer, Hesiod, Heraclitus, Euripides, and Aristophanes, Nietzsche's aesthetic differentiation of Apollonian and Dionysian elements seems to be particularly helpful; in this book, these oppositional elements (provoking either cosmological order or chaos) serve as analytic tools to explore the meanings of playfulness in the archaic life-world.

Homer's and Hesiod's works mark ludic beginnings in Western thought. They stand both for being major works that survived into posterity and for providing critical fodder for such varied thinkers as Heraclitus, Plato, and Aristotle. For instance, Heraclitus faults both of them for inciting superstition and sentimentality in their respective audiences by invoking a mythic, heroic past. Euripides and Aristophanes, too, return to the mythic Hellenic nobles but differ in their depictions of "proper play." Since I share Michel Foucault and Judith Butler's suspicion of origins, I wish to concentrate on the above mentioned poets and thinkers as Beispiele (examples)[3] for my purposes here—but not in order to demonstrate that one can pinpoint a particular idea which originates a school of thought on play. Rather, I am interested in studying the effects of the shift from a play-affirming perspective to a decisively disapproving ethical attitude towards play.

Much has been written about this shift, but mostly with respect to Plato's introduction of art as mimesis and the eclipse of Hellenic tragedy in the fifth century B.C. Major ludic shifts occur in the works of Hesiod and Aristophanes. By ridiculing Euripides' tragic plays as "feminized" (i.e., trivial) in *The Frogs*, Aristophanes dispenses with some of Dionysus's masks. There is a lack of both moralism and realism in Euripides' tragic play world, which I wish to contrast with Aristophanes's harsh moralist attack of Euripides' naturalist representation in *The Frogs*. Hence, Aristophanes's critique inaugurates an important ludic shift: Apollonian logos predominates over Dionysian frenzy. Aristophanes's comedies—not Euripides' tragedies—bring on the demise of the Dionysian play. In order to trace this development of the valences of Dionysian and Apollonian play elements, let us first turn to ludic performativities in the archaic world.

Agonism in Homer's World

Homer's ludic world is full of uninhibited exuberance and violence. Agonistic play dominates—the rule of the game simply is might makes right. Homer's heroes carry out war games (*aristeia*), battling for life or death; their motto is: "Always be best and excel others" (*Iliad* 6, 208).[4] Homer's play is, above all, a (deadly) play of the archaic noble, aided and abetted by the quarrelsome gods; thus it is a play that hangs on fate/chance, depending on the particular divine intervention. There is no self-chosen rational *kairos* (a favorable time—to engage an opponent and come out victorious). The gods are the puppet masters, as the Stranger tells us glumly in Plato's *Laws*. This divine game controls the horizon (fate) of the player. It is not up to a heroic noble (Achilles) or a young princess (Nausicaa) to determine the conditions or rules of their game. However, this cosmic chance-game prescribed for the heroes (and others) is not deterministic;

the Homeric human players are not always already cast as innocent or ignorant, i.e., as being devoid of reason and decision making.

Spariosu (1991) contrasts Homer's archaic (agonistic) concept of having power over someone with Hesiod's "median" (cooperative, nonagonistic) notion of power. Hesiod's play thus radically transforms the nature of play: it no longer provokes violence but is thoroughly rational, fair play.[5] Given this shift, Spariosu suggests that it is necessary to supplement the Nietzschean aesthetic principles (Apollonian and Dionysian) with a different set of opposites, namely archaic and median values, which better addresses the issue of power in play. Borrowing from a famous passage of the *Iliad* and drawing on Nietzsche's *Philosophy in the Tragic Age of the Greeks*, he states:

> This Homeric notion of play as arbitrary, free, and effortless movement analogous to a god's or a child's activity becomes a philosophical principle for the first time in Heraclitus. . . . The Homeric simile also implicitly opposes the effortlessness and freedom of play with the painful constraint of work. . . . Apollo's aristeia highlights the difference between archaic play and games of an orderly, median nature: a god, like a child, can invent games to amuse himself, and as such he can create an orderly, rule-governed world ("sand-towers"); as soon as he gets bored, however, still playing, he may destroy this world and start building a new one according to different rules for no other reason than the sheer pleasure of the game.[6]

While it is plausible to address the issues of power in playful activities in the way that Spariosu offers to do, it is not convincing to limit the expression of agonism, of competitiveness, and violence to the Archaic Age, and the notion of fair play to the Classical Age. He argues that median values appear in Plato's discussion of child's play: "paidia comes to denote not only 'children's play' but also 'play' in general. It is the moment when philosophy separates play from agon, that is, from violent contest and power."[7] Yet, the archaic sense of power is conspicuously absent from the leisurely or peaceful games in honor of the gods in the *Iliad*. Spariosu also oscillates in his descriptions of protorational thought; both Heraclitus and Hesiod tend to subscribe to median values, even though it is really the logocentric tradition, beginning with Plato, which ushers in the median conception of play and power.

What then is the nature of play in the Homeric world? Even though the term *paidia* is absent from the Homeric epos, Homer does comment on children's playfulness, as pointed out by Spariosu. Besides the sand tower simile, which can be subjected to multiple interpretations with respect to the role of a boy child, Homer has in store more negative comments on the inadequacy of children and of women: Warriors should not let themselves get intimidated like a feeble child [*pais aphauros*] or a woman (*Il.* 7, 235), and a man should not babble nonsense as a child would do (*Od.* 4, 32).[8]

This negative portrayal of children in particular does not explain, however, the role of Apollo, god of warfare, who is compared to a child sweeping away the sand tower it just created. This simile does not conjure up the image of innocence cherished by modern popular child psychology which pronounces the infant incapable of discerning good and evil. Instead, it invokes a sense of capriciousness and reckless joy. These attributes of childlike Apollo may not have a negative ring for the Homeric poets as they would for Hesiod or Plato. Is a child's and god's play always already agonistic, though? Let us take a closer look at the passage in question. Fagles translates:

> Holding formation now the Trojans rolled across [the trench], / Apollo heading them, gripping the awesome storm-shield / and he tore that Argive rampart down with the same ease / some boy at the seashore knocks sand castles down— / he no sooner builds his playthings [*athurmata*] up, child's play [*nepieesin*], / than he wrecks them all with hands and kicking feet, / just for the sport of it. God of the wild cry, Apollo— / so you wrecked the Achaeans' work and drove the men / who had built it up with all that grief and labor / into headlong panic rout. (*Il.* 15, 360-67)

Among German translators, interpretations of the Homeric child's play varies, ranging from a derogatory validation of "childishness" (*mit kindischem Sinn*)[9] to a more neutral interpretation of "a childlike pleasure" (*in kindlicher Freude*).[10] The boyish sport spells disaster, though; the poet rebukes Apollo for erasing the product of toil of the Achaeans. Divine playful capriciousness triumphs over human hard labor.[11] In this context play clearly has an agonistic, destructive connotation. Spariosu does, however, concede a shift from archaic to median values in the *Odyssey*, for we can observe that upon his arrival at home Odysseus's identity changes from a warrior to a country gentleman,[12] which indicates a shift of values from unscrupulous cunning to becoming a peace-loving negotiator. Yet, for the most part, the Homeric epos is determined by archaic values. But one may want to refrain from the temptation of suggesting that one era's literature has a more violent character than another era, which, by contrast, is deemed more "civilized," such as the Classical Age of Plato and Socrates.[13] This is a superficial assessment and leads to a romanticization of the epoch that is cast as the deviant Other.[14]

In addition to describing the Homeric epos as exuding prerational, violent archaic values, commentators have also construed his world as truly "innocent," representing a pure, naive, childlike perspective. Erich Auerbach's analysis is exemplary in engaging in such idealization of innocence. In his book *Mimesis: The Representation of Reality in Western Literature* (1953), Auerbach contrasts Homer's representation of reality (i.e., mimesis) with that of the Elohist of the Old Testament in the powerfully written chapter "Odysseus' Scar." The contrast is especially compelling given Auerbach's shrewd analysis of the different syntactical structure of the two texts; the complex syntax used by the Elohist reflects on the multifaceted, enigmatic character of Abraham, whereas the simple compound structure of the Homeric prose gives a more naturalistic portrayal of the heroes and their environments.

Delight in physical existence is everything to [the Homeric poems], and their highest aim is to make that delight perceptible to us. Between battles and passions, adventures and perils, they show us hunts, banquets, palaces and shepherds' cots, athletic contests and washing days—in order that we may see the heroes in their ordinary life, and seeing them so, may take pleasure in their manner of enjoying their savory present, a present which sends strong roots down into social usages, landscape, and daily life. And thus they bewitch us and ingratiate themselves to us until we live with them in the reality of their lives; so long as we are reading or hearing the poems, it does not matter whether we know that all this is only legend, "make-believe."[15]

Homer's heroes are delightfully simple. Although Auerbach refrains from calling them innocent, he notes that they act as if they start living their lives every morning anew and without anguish vis-à-vis the gods—in contradistinction to the anxiety-stricken Abraham in the Elohist's story. The Hellenic nobles lead a life of leisure and eternal bliss, not complicated by ethical questions, such as the ones faced by Abraham. Homer paints a picture of reality that exists for its own sake, leading Auerbach to the following comment: "Homer can be analyzed . . . but he cannot be interpreted."[16] He concludes that Homer fails in holding the reader in suspense and fails in painting a more complex psychological picture of his heroes.

What does this have to do with Homer's treatment of play and contests? While Auerbach's analysis perhaps adequately depicts the tragic characters in the *Iliad*, I contend that the *Odyssey* is imbued with a sense of humanity, of versatile human behavior that is at the same time an inherently fateful, tragic play.[17] Auerbach's critique of Homer's naturalism, which portrays phenomena as lacking "a glimpse of unplumbed depths," ultimately leads to a characterization of the Hellenic play as being shallow and lacking a complex subjective perspective; Homer's nobles simply enjoy "their savory present." Auerbach claims this naturalist portrayal reduces humans to simpletons who live for no other purpose than play and contests. This kind of playful attitude towards a life which is nonserious is maligned in Auerbach's deliberate juxtaposition of the light and descriptive Homeric verses with the passage of Abraham's sacrifice of Isaac, which is full of seriousness, suspense, and grave silence: clearly, life is not merely about play but about leading a purposeful existence and pondering life-and-death decisions.

Yet, to claim that Achilles and Agamemnon cherish "childish" play is to read certain passages of the *Iliad* against the current. The nobles are admonished to assume a proper play pose—not to play, to act as children do (*Iliad*, 7.401). Children, after all, cannot distinguish between words and deeds; they are easily frightened by mere verbal insults (cf. 20.200-58).[18] These passages seem to have little in common with the famous sand tower simile in Book 15 (15.361), which portrays the gods intervening in human matters with a certain lightness—like a child, being at ease, playing in the sand, randomly building and destroying sand towers, just for the fun of it. However, there are different standards of "propriety" for gods and humans. In fact, the contrast between serious, struggling heroes and buffoon-like gods could not be painted in starker colors in the *Iliad*. Fränkel (1975) points out that the play and laughter of the gods is unrestrained; they exchange vulgar jokes and rejoice at the sight of the nasty and brutish human existence: "[W]hen men fight for life and death, the gods join in as a joke and Zeus' heart laughs for joy at their strife."[19] Achilles's rage may be deemed childlike, irrational, hubristic, but his posture is heroic, because he is determined to set the rules to his game—not to be swayed by the bribes of Agamemnon, the Greek commander-in-chief, who needs to lure Achilles back into the battle against Hector's victorious army. Even though Homer's heroes are objects of play—as the child simile suggests—rather than its masters or subjects, they behave as if they can avoid the divine puppeteers.

In the *Odyssey* the depiction of playfulness is also varied and complex. Here, too, one can take issue with Auerbach's theory that the Homeric style, elegant as it may be, lacks a perspective of depth when it comes to describing human interactions. Prima facie it seems that play has only bucolic features: it is sweet (Book 23) and radiant, Nausicaa's ball game excites the gods, notably the nymphs "of field and forest" (Book 6), and it gives delight to warriors, as Odysseus's contest with the Phaeacians (Book 8) and the suitors' games at Odysseus's homestead attest to (cf. Books 1, 17, 21).

However, the spirit of play in the *Odyssey* is not captured by derogatory or diminutive connotations of superficiality, innocence, and self-indulgence. Not all of the games are autotelic, i.e., played for their own sake. I will argue that they are used for an interplay of Apollonian and Dionysian power, e.g., for tactical, cunning distractions, for diversionary strategies (masking real purposes, e.g., the plan to murder the suitors). However, the Homeric poets invoke a prohibition of a special kind of mimetic play: imitating the gods leads to hubris. Nevertheless, it is difficult to discern a unitary picture of the use of play in this epic work because of different narrative styles employed by the Homeric poets.

As Schadewaldt notes in the epilogue of his translation of the *Odyssey*, there are clear clues to suggest that two poets compiled the epic.[20] The older version (A) encompasses about two thirds of the text. It is "hohe Dichtung,"[21] i.e., its composition is well-rounded with only a few figures, limited descriptions, and few speeches. Version (B) is quite different from that. It gives an elaborate, rational account of why Odysseus is compelled to slay the suitors: they have to be burdened with guilt. So in B, the suitors plan to kill Odysseus's son Telemachus. In addition, the B version paints a more realistic picture of politics and customs at the aristocratic home of Odysseus.

In Book 1 poet B gives an ominous rendition of the games of the suitors in order to forewarn us about the men's immediate doom (which however is delayed till the Book 23). While enjoying their dice game the suitors are characterized as *agenoras* (23, 106), i.e., as arrogant braggarts, and scolded for the ease with which they sing and dance and force the bard Phemious to play the lyre for them. Interestingly, poet B imitates poet A in anticipation of Odysseus's use of the words *anathemata daitos* (setting up the feast) in Book 21 which gives the cue for the slaughter of the suitors.[22] We can infer that poet B clearly disapproves of the pastime and sportive diversions of the suitors. In contrast to their reckless behavior, poet B gives us a detailed account of Odysseus's good competitive play at the Phaeacians. Odysseus accepts Laodamas's bait to play; he shows the Phaeacians how to play well, i.e., he introduces the notion of fair play being played for its own sake. This Apollonian "fair play" nevertheless has a good deal of agonistic posturing.

Poet A stresses the functional aspect of play. "Fair play," as I see it, is absent. Even the incident of Nausicaa and her maids' leisurely ball game, which is often cited to show that Homer treats games as having ends in themselves, is not really played for savory delight. The game is mainly set up to ensure that Odysseus is discovered by a princess, Nausicaa, and taken to her parents' castle. Athena intervenes in the ball game so that Nausicaa's (play)mate fails to catch the ball, which falls into the adjacent river, where Odysseus rests and awakens from the women's shrieks (6, 100-115).

Games played for their own sake are not always condoned. The suitors are judged to be vain, arrogant, and indulging contestants. This interpretation becomes even clearer at the climactic moment at the end of Book 21 where Odysseus, disguised as a beggar, facetiously invites the suitors to engage in leisure activities, such as dance or chants and playing the lyre, "since those are the ornaments of a feast" (21, 429-30). Little do they know that they are about to be killed and burnt as a sacrifice to the gods for transgressing basic rules of Hellenic hospitality. So Odysseus's command to start the play is only a cue for his son to seize the weapons and begin the massacre.

This is not to say that games in the *Odyssey* do not have a serious meaning; on the contrary, they are holy, fateful, and have to be played with the right attitude, namely, to be unpretentious and humble towards the gods and the host. The repeated negative descriptions of the suitors' play are Homer's stern warning to uphold the sacrosanct order of play. In some sense, to violate this order is to gamble with one's death, i.e., to play with one's hubris. Playing can also be a life-threatening activity and not simply a savory, delightful event! And playing and jesting at the wrong time, disobeying one's kairos, is especially fateful, as we know from Odysseus's facetious and provocative outburst at the blinded Cyclops that led to the death of his comrades and his own twenty-year-long wandering (Book 9, 474-505).

In Book 23, poet B gives an account of social games being played perfunctorily in order to distract from other trickery. Having spilt lots of the blood of the suitors, Odysseus invites his kin to play triumphantly in order to create the perception for the outside world that his wife has finally accepted a proposition and is celebrating her wedding with a suitor; Odysseus wants to buy more time before the kin of the slain sons and brothers pursue the avenger. Performing revelling dances (cf. 23, 134) after such enormous bloodshed may under other circumstances be a bad display of arrogance and hubris, but here it is perhaps a necessary act of purification. Odysseus is aware of hubris and appeals to the pious sentiments of the aged Euryclea by admonishing her not to rejoice loudly when she witnesses the slaughter.

To sum up the contrasts between the two versions vis-à-vis play and games, poet A's account of play lacks the lightness and purposelessness which poet B emphasizes. For instance, in Book 17, poet A describes the suitors' play with discus and javelins as being insolent. He issues a stern warning against transgressing the world order, i.e., of shamelessly occupying Odysseus's *oikos*; committing such an act of transgression entails the certainty of imminent punishment. Poet B simply parrots this in Book 1 but—without mentioning hubris—

his mimicry of poet A fails to attain the graveness of the situation; similarly in the above mentioned passage in Book 23 mockery (of hubris) seems to dominate, but it is more ambiguous because in the end Odysseus's actions lead us to believe that piety prevails over ostentatious cunning.

Clearly, an analysis of key passages in the *Odyssey* and the *Iliad* ought to illustrate that the conception of play in Homer's epos is multifaceted, rather than one-dimensional. It cannot be done justice by characterizing it either as shallow and simple (Auerbach) or as prerational (Spariosu). However, what might lead somebody like Auerbach to the observation that Homer's nobles have a displaced joie de vivre could be attributed to the poets' downplaying of the importance of work. Toiling does not seem to be a part of the aristocratic way of life as narrated in the Homeric epics and the later dramaturgists and thinkers—perhaps with the exception of Hesiod's *Works and Days*—which leads Spariosu to the following assertion: "Even during the classical period and later [. . .], in Aristotle's discussion of schole (leisure, play), diagoge (diversion), paidia (play), and ascholia (occupation, work), it is play rather than work that produces most Hellenic values."[23] Some play theoreticians have been prone to romanticization of this (ideological) production of cultural values. In his famous play study Johan Huizinga succumbs to this trap by asserting emphatically that the archaic Greek society was a "playful society."[24] To be sure, the act of designing the blueprints for the Parthenon may involve leisure; however, actually carting the stones and building the structure is hardly a playful amusement.

Let us turn to a different conception of play proposed by Hesiod, a self-proclaimed farmer and poet.

Toying with Fair Play in Hesiod

Hesiod wrote around 700 BC but was considered a contemporary of Homer by later generations (e.g., by Herodotus).[25] The most popular and influential works of his that have survived in complete form are the *Theogony* (hereafter *Theog.*) and the *Works and Days* (*W&D*).[26]

Spariosu holds that Hesiod's discussion of play constitutes a dramatic departure from the Homeric representation of archaic play. What is novel is the emergence of a different logos of play, namely Hesiod's introduction of fair play (among mortals) and median notions of power, best articulated in the famous fable of the hawk and the nightingale (cf. *W&D* 202-12). This idea is absent for the most part from the Homeric epos, where heroes win by being favorites of gods and goddesses who lend a helping hand in extending the length of their hero's spear throw. No such guarantee of divine intervention is promised in Hesiod's poems.

To be sure, Hesiod expresses much contempt for deceitful actions and extols the virtue of a "straight logos." Yet, Hesiod does not altogether abandon the archaic ways of playing, i.e., of "crooked logos." His diction, as one commentator puts it, "loves the unexpected, loves dramatic contrasts and foiled anticipations."[27] One such noteworthy example is the Muses' song in the opening passages of the *Theogony*. It displays Hesiod's ironic stance towards his own profession; he chides fellow shepherds (possibly also the Homeric poets) as being all too susceptible to the trickery of the Muses' *logoi*:[28]

> Shepherds of the fields, poor fools, mere bellies!
> We [the Muses] know how to say many lies similar [or identical] to true things,
> but if we want, we know how to sing the truth. (*Theog.* 26ff.)[29]

Such cunning is unprecedented in the Archaic era, for Hesiod challenges the idea that the Muses' song, i.e., poetry, is about uttering truth.[30] The Muses reveal to Hesiod that their sweet sayings may be at times laced with a crooked account, which imitates perfectly straight logos.[31] The Muses' make-believe cannot be deciphered by Hesiod's fellow poets, derogatorily called "poor fools, mere bellies." However, since Hesiod has to be "taught" (*Theog.* 22) this revelation, i.e., he does not independently acquire this insight, he can barely escape the Muses' stinging attack himself. "Authentic" truth is hardly distinct from truth which is imitated; in fact, it is Hesiod who is susceptible to the cunning wit of the Muses, because they prompt a displacement of logos.[32] Still, given the ambiguity of the passage, another reading is possible: it shows Hesiod's ironic self-deprecating attitude and flirtation with Dionysian play—perhaps the ability to laugh at himself (insofar as this kind of mockery is plausible for such a stern poet). Even though emphatically denying that he is much like the Homeric poets, Hesiod perhaps secretly knows that it is even impossible for him to receive only the straight logos, unadulterated from crooked falsehoods.[33] The "divine voice" that is "breathed" into him (31) may just turn out to be a fake ploy by the cunning Muses. Lamberton's reading seems to go in this direction as well, noting that the Muses' truth-telling is a "play of poses, a complex and implicating system of representation that constantly tantalizes us with the possibility that it represents something."[34]

Hesiod also departs from the Homeric tradition with respect to the creationist story of Prometheus, "the devious planner" (*Theog.* 521) who is trying to outsmart Zeus; here the notion of fair play is irrelevant because Zeus demands absolute loyalty; he determines the dice throw. Prometheus's cunning and trickery earn him eternal bondage, and, since he allies himself with mortal men, Zeus brings about the "baneful" creation of women, conceived as bringing evil and being "conspirers in troublesome works." Hesiod impresses upon his reader/listener the stern warning that nobody may deceive and toy with Zeus's wit without encountering a terrible fate (*Theog.* 535-616).

The *Works and Days* repeats the Prometheus story but introduces another misogynist element: an irate Zeus orders the other deities to create a duplicitous figure, "an evil to love and embrace" called Pandora ("the gift of all"—a gift by all the gods to men).[35] Pandora is made out of clay and water, but she is not merely a plaything of the gods; simulating a goddess Pandora carries out her own cunning deeds (*W&D* 60 ff.). Her double identity (bringer of mischief as well as fleeting enjoyment) displaces the (straight) logos of truth, as we have already seen in the case of the Muses. Truth is simulated truth and thus plays with the "crooked" logos. Pandora's mission is to carry out Zeus's fateful game to spoil the paradisical human condition forever; bios, the livelihood of men, i.e., the good life (of leisure), is kept hidden from humans (*W&D* 42-46). Pandora brings misery in the form of burdensome labor and painful diseases and marks the advent of women who devise "anguishing miseries for men" (91-92). She serves as Zeus's revenge, as antidote, to Prometheus's cunning devising. This duplicitous pair, Prometheus and Pandora, foreshadows Dionysus, the god of many masquerades.[36] In Hesiod's works, though, this god is simply named as "bringer of joy" and as a god of wine; nothing is said about the nature of the Dionysian cult. Yet, I would argue, because Hesiod is both fascinated and repelled by a crooked logos, we see traces of Dionysian playfulness in his poems.

Hesiod also invokes tragic, Dionysian play in his discussion of work. Hard labor—not play and leisure—is the scattered content of Pandora's jar (*W&D* 95), which, coupled with strife, encompasses the human condition. In the *Theogony*, which is a creationist account of the Greek deities, the goddess Night gives birth to bad Eris (strife, discord), "a hard-hearted demon" from whom descend "[c]onflicts of Battle and Fights and Murders and Killings of Men, Quarrels and Lies and Words [*logoi!*] and Disputations, Disorderly Government and her accomplice, the power of Ruin . . ." (*Theog.,* 226-30). This dramatic enumeration of images without the use of copulae evokes associations with the loathsome vision of the state of nature as outlined in Hobbes's *Leviathan.*[37] Such wretchedness, such a colossal breakdown of the social order, the lack of fair play, dominates Hesiod's own life, which is allegorically alluded to in the account of the iron race in *Work and Days*—rules of the game are broken to further one's own advantage:

> Might will be justice; and one will destroy the other's city. Neither will he who swears truly be favored nor he who is just nor he who is good, but he will be granted promotion to honor who is a doer of evil and hubris. Might will be justice and shame will no longer exist. The bad will injure the good, speaking crooked untruths and bearing false witness thereto. (*W&D* 189-94)

Yet, alternatives to such a crude might makes right account of justice could be envisioned—and here we see the introduction of an ontological distinction of different types of play. In the beginning of *Works and Days*, Hesiod alludes to "good" Eris, the good spirit of peaceful competition, who is clearly in opposition to the hubristic Eris (cf. *W&D,* 11 ff.). Hekate[38] is praised as bringing luck to athletes who compete in the games and brings fortune to farmers and fishers, when they call upon her. Like the Muses, she too is a capricious figure, capable of denying luck to mortals if she wills to do so (*Theog.* 435-45). Note the importance of chance-play for Hesiod (it is also important for Homer and Heraclitus). Gods in the archaic world are not predictable, but humans can hope that they are favorable to their plight—by fearing the gods. *Elpis* (hope or fear), which was not scattered but remains in Pandora's jar tightly sealed, is the only (positive) element which Zeus leaves for humans to control (*W&D* 96-99). Hesiod introduces two notions of play, where one is praised as a lawful play in accord with orderliness and piety while the other is maligned as a play of the mighty and ruthless, a play of spoilsports who toy with hubris. Both notions are infused with elements of competitiveness as the link with Strife indicates.

The notion of fair play, i.e., Apollonian play, is perhaps best illustrated in the fable of the Hawk and Nightingale (*W&D* 202-12).[39] Fair play is postulated as "straight" play, as is shown in the analogy of both the nightingale and dike being dragged off by unjust actors (kings, bribed judges, etc.). Another example of good strife is depicted in the following famous expression:

> Neighbor is envious of neighbor
> hastening to wealth, and this is the Eris that benefits mortals.
> Potter fiercely challenges potter, carpenter carpenter,
> beggar enviously strives with beggar, singer with singer. (*W&D* 23-26)

But is good and bad strife always cast as opposition? As I noted above, Hesiod incurs a nasty sting against his competitors in the Muses' song. I concur with Pucci who notes that competition (=good strife) and discord (=bad strife) are posed as an empty polarity because it seems quite arbitrary to judge what counts as good or bad strife.[40] So rather than casting Eris as oppositional, I suggest that we regard this pair as characterizing different degrees of agonistic Eris.

Play *qua paidia* does not appear in these poems; on the other hand, the ode "Exhortation of Work" (286-319) introduces the opposites of work and (foolish) idleness in moral terms of *arete* vs. *kakotes*, reflecting Hesiod's bitterness at being wronged by his (lazy) brother Peseus, who sued him in court over his inheritance. Hesiod thus comes across as the spoilsport of the ontological priority of play and leisure. An ode to work is alien to Homer's worldview and to other Greek thinkers of the archaic epoch. Hesiod, an independently successful farmer, condemns the warrior-class and the aristocrats who administer "crooked" justice (like the hawk holding the feeble nightingale "by the grip of his bent talons," 212); thus he prioritizes the order of the household [*oikos*] and agriculture over the city-dwellers of the warriors;[41] this is also expressed in the pastoral style and content of his poems.

Hesiod differs from Homer insofar as he extolls the virtues of work as something willed by the gods. He introduces fair play (Apollonian play) with the notion of the good Eris and is critical of warrior-like agonistic Eris. Yet, even though Hesiod endorses "straight" justice over a "crooked" one, he does not play by those rules consistently, as is illustrated by the song of the Muses in the *Theogony* and by the Prometheus-Pandora story in *Work and Days* where he toys with Dionysian play. Again, Spariosu's notions of prerational versus rational values do not capture the kind of play Hesiod advocates; this is illustrated, too, in the depictions of the apparently different kinds of strife that cannot be as neatly separated as he imagined.

Heraclitus's Human Play World

Both Homer and Hesiod are in some sense antipodes to Heraclitus of Ephesus, a contemporary of Parmenides. Critical of Hesiod's espousal of superstitions

(B57), Heraclitus also indicts Homer, who, he says, "deserves to be thrown out of the competitions and deserves to take a beating" (B42). Heraclitus's contempt probably stems from the anthropomorphic treatment of the divine in the Homeric epics, which is echoed in several fragments ridiculing the practice of religious rites (cf. B5, B14, B15). In fragment B15, in particular, he critiques his fellow citizens for their worship of Dionysus, who, after all, is not only a god of procreation but also the god of death, Hades:[42]

> If it were not in honor of Dionysus that they conducted the procession, and sang the phallic hymn, their activity would be completely shameless. But Hades is Dionysus, in whose honor they rave and perform the Bacchic revels. (B15)

As Fränkel (1975) puts it in jest, Heraclitus wants to point out that "the fools may continue in wild intoxication to hail their own deaths."[43] However, despite his ridicule of the prevalent religious beliefs and practices, Heraclitus, no doubt, takes play, especially Dionysian play, very seriously. This sentiment is particularly manifest in fr. B52.

The famous fragment B52[44] anchors Heraclitus's conception of play. Perhaps it is the ultimate expression of cunning and elusive playfulness, since its meaning can never be completely gathered up. It is the Achilles heel of every philosophical play theory. The fragment says: "Lifetime is a child at play, moving pieces in a game. Kingship belongs to the child."[45] In the philosophical reception of this fragment, five interpretations dominate: (1) the significance of a cosmic play where gods and humans are in an ecstatic relation to the cosmic fire (Nietzsche 1962; Fink 1960); (2) the game is determined by calculated rules (Kahn 1979); (3) an agonism drives the rules (Spariosu 1991); (4) appearance of arbitrary rules, yet the game is determined by the gods (Fränkel 1960); and (5) the child is *aion* (life) and bearer of Apollo and Dionysus who play with mortals (Wohlfart 1991).

Eugen Fink (1960) suggests that the play of humans has cosmic significance. "Both gods and men are in an ecstatic relation to pyr and aion, their poetic force rests in play of the world."[46] Fink maintains that in the post-Heraclitean era, there is a distancing between gods and humans, which he determines as the beginning of Western metaphysics. However, he notes that Plato asserts that the relationship between the gods and humans is play insofar as the mortal becomes a plaything of the god (*paignon theou*).[47] Fink echoes Nietzsche's concatenation of fire and cosmic force; however, Nietzsche also insists on the play's character of "innocent caprice" and invokes the sand castle image of the *Iliad*, thus combining creatively play metaphors from Homer and Heraclitus:

> In this world only play, play as artists and children engage in it, exhibits coming-to-be and passing away, structuring and destroying, without any moral additive, in forever equal innocence. And as children and artists play, so plays the ever-lasting fire. It constructs and destroys, all in innocence. Such is the game that the aeon plays with itself. Transforming itself into water and earth, it builds towers of sand like a child at the seashore, piles them up and tramples them down. From time to time it starts the game anew. . . . Not hubris but the

ever self-renewing impulse to play calls new worlds into being. The child throws its toys away from time to time—and starts again, in innocent caprice. But when it does build, it combines and joins and forms its structures regularly, conforming to inner laws. (Nietzsche 1962, 62; emphasis added)

While Nietzsche captures the image of becoming and perishing as laws of life (the *aion*), he also affirms that the child's play has a certain naivety, an innocence, which makes possible the harmonious interplay of Apollonian regularity and Dionysian capricious impulses.

Hermann Fränkel (1960) speculates that the chess-playing child makes up rules arbitrarily; it is a random, human rule-governed game, comparable to the one in Plato (*Laws*, 803c-804b) where humans are playthings of gods. Fränkel notes that fr. B52 with its focus on fallible, unpredictable human law finds its pendant in the higher, divine law, mentioned in B114: "For all human laws get nourishment from the one divine law." This can only mean, Fränkel argues, that Reason is not an accomplishment of an individual but relies on a superhuman universal power.[48] In a later work Fränkel (1975) refines his position and claims that the cryptic fragment gives hints about the ethical choices of humans. The outcome of human actions is determined by the gods, since "[i]t would not be good for men if all that they desire took place" (cf. B110). Thus, he states that it is not surprising if "our life plays games with us according to equally arbitrary rules."[49]

Instead of reflecting on children's "innocence," Fränkel points out that in Heraclitus's times, children were considered weak or feebleminded creatures.[50] Childhood is nothing but a preliminary stage to maturity.[51] Only much later, during Christianity, a child's "positive" values were discovered. To be sure, children in the Hellenic age were not highly valued, but it is misleading to suggest that they were not appreciated at all. While Fränkel provides an important corrective of Nietzschean romanticism, his analysis lacks adequate appreciation of Heraclitus's "child" metaphor. After all, several fragments point to children's ability to outwit the wisest of all men, Homer, with a simple riddle (B56). B121 encapsulates Heraclitus's ironic advice to the citizens of Ephesus, who should let their children rule them, because they seem much less "despicable" than the corrupt adults.[52]

Mihai Spariosu asserts that Heraclitus's play is a "restless play of warring forces," since elsewhere in the fragments play is compared to strife (*polemos*, *eris*) and thus has nothing of the "innocence of a child's play." Furthermore, Spariosu rejects Kahn's (1979) rationalistic explanation that the child's moves follow definite, calculated rules. Kahn argues that it makes little sense talking about random play, since the fragment mentions *pesseuon* [moving pieces]; in order to play *pessoi*, a board game such as backgammon which involves dice, a player has to move the counters following definite rules, such as alternating in turns. Clearly, the act of playing against an imaginary other is an important aspect of children's pretend-play. Yet, Kahn draws the following conclusion: "The rules of the pessoi-game thus imitate the alternating measures of cosmic fire."[53] Kahn's leap from an anthropocentric play to a cosmological order of things seems to be unsupported by his analysis.

Günter Wohlfart (1991) devotes an entire book to the notorious fragment B52 and has advanced the scholarly treatment of the fragment significantly. He notes that Heraclitus adapts Homeric similes, notably the *Iliad*'s child's play simile (Book 15, 360 ff.), although he alters the Apollonian game (*athurmata*) of building and confounding "sand heaps" (i.e., the Argives's sand rampart) to the imagery of playing at draughts. However, Wohlfart claims that *sugcheo* (to confound), which does not literally appear in B52, plays an analogous role in the fragment, because the Heraclitean boy also "confounds" his opponent in the *pessoi*-game by building obstacles (as suggested by modern games, such as *Tavli* [Greek], *Tric-Trac* [French], and—I would add—*Malefitz* [German]).[54] In Homer, pais qua Apollo confounds the toil of humans; analogously, in Heraclitus, *pais* qua *aion* (life) toys with the mortals. Plato seems to have combined both images, hinting at the playful lightness (characterizing both god and boy) of Homer's simile and the board player (*petteute*) of Heraclitus's simile.[55] Most interpretations of B52 seem to be at loss over the comparison of the child with *basileus* (king). Wohlfart puts forth several compelling interpretations, first, equating pais with Apollo, then Dionysus, and thirdly, with the fate of Kyros, the Persian king (according to Herodotus, Kyros, supposedly a shepherd's son, was elected king as a child during a game [of *basilinda*] and actually ends up ruling over his archenemy King Astyages, thus reversing the power dynamic: the Persians become masters, the Medes, slaves).[56] Those who are children today (worthless) are kings tomorrow. The lot given to each of us may be turned around by chance-play.[57]

In my view, this game is mastered equally by the (adult) king and child. Heraclitus does not differentiate between the skills of the child and those of the adult; furthermore, the child's play is not romanticized; it has nothing to do with innocence. Drawing on Wohlfart's interpretation, the child's regal persona toys with both Dionysian and Apollonian masquerade. Taking off the mask would merely reveal another mask.[58] I also agree with Kahn's focus on the imagery of "playing with draughts," instead of speculating on the psyche of children. But he does not look at the chance/hazard part—Kahn puts too much emphasis into the role of *ananke*. Fränkel (1975) is correct to stress the role of chance but does so at the expense of *ananke*; furthermore he does not properly assess the role of children: a board game played by a child may seem irrational and nonsensical to an adult, who observes the moves of the player, but perhaps, Heraclitus is eager here to "confound," to toy with, his adult audience, who does not grasp the orderly, rule-directed moves of the child which in fact are not randomly executed at all. Furthermore, as Heraclitus puts it, mistakes are deeds of humans (B70), suggesting that humans are not mere playthings of gods but responsible for their actions.

Perhaps a better perspective is to take Heraclitus's mantra, the unity of opposites, to task: This play of *aion* is a struggle of chance and necessity, the interplay of the Dionysian and Apollonian forces. A divine decision is necessarily fateful but humans choose their fate by "taking their mistaken views as seriously as children their toys" (B70). Another way of interpreting this interplay dialectically is using Nietzsche's formulation of "law in becoming" and "play in necessity" (Nietzsche 1962, 68).

What are some sociopolitical implications of Heraclitus's play? Spariosu accuses Heraclitus's play of being thoroughly elitist and blames it on his aristocratic origins. Although I do not want to dismiss his point, he perhaps overstates his case by charging that for Heraclitus only aristocratic play is worth of consideration. After all, boys, even of ignoble origins, are considered being at least of equal worth (e.g., in the case of outsmarting Homer). Spariosu's point is well taken, though, with respect to Heraclitus's grudges against *hoi polloi*. "The many" simply do not have the leisure, the freedom to forgo hard work, in order to play. Still, I maintain that Heraclitus's thought is motivated by the doctrine of the unity of opposites and does not necessarily imply that only nobles know how to play well—unlike Aristotle's normative move, who will charge that only the play of the philosophers, the true nobles, is valuable in itself. However, this child's play is essentially monological or solitary, which has no need for performing with or for others. In modern terminology, Heraclitus posits a self's inner struggle with oppositional forces. Heraclitus's play is thus the specter haunting modern and postmodern plays of the self.

Euripides and Aristophanes: The Role of Dionysus in Greek Mythos

Turning to poetic representations of play in the classical period, let us focus on Euripides and Aristophanes who figure as transitional "players," insofar as Euripides is more sympathetic to Dionysian frenzy in his tragic plays while Aristophanes leans toward an Apollonian, orderly, and rationalistic perspective. The examples used to underscore these claims are *The Bacchae* and *The Frogs*.

In the second part of Aristophanes' play *The Frogs*, Dionysus is called in to preside as judge over the contest between Euripides and Aeschylus over which one deserves Sophocles' chair in Hades. Whoever beats all his rivals in each of the great sciences and liberal arts will eat at the Prytaneum and take a seat at Pluto's side. Aeagus tells Dionysus that he needs to preside over the dispute, since he is the master of tragic poetry. Dionysus's rhetorical mastery is nicely displayed by Aristophanes when the god of masks mocks Euripides' poetry: A boastful Euripides "introduces our private life upon the stage, our common habits."

> 'Tis thus that I taught my audience how to judge, namely, by introducing the art of reasoning and considering into tragedy. Thanks to me, they understand everything, discern all things, conduct their households better and ask themselves, 'What is to be thought of this? Where is that? Who has taken the other thing?'

Dionysus retorts in mockery:

> Yes certainly, and now every Athenian who returns home, bawls to his slaves, 'Where is the stew-pot? Who has eaten off the sprat's head? Where is the clove of garlic that was left over from yesterday? Who has been nibbling at my ol-

ives?' Whereas formerly they kept their seats with mouths agape like fools and idiots. (971-91)

Aristophanes derides Euripides for having denigrated Greek tragedy by introducing the banalities of daily life onto the stage.[59] However, I contend that one should not readily dismiss Euripides' depiction of the "tragic mask" of Dionysus. Spariosu says it aptly in the following quote by alluding to the Nietzschean "iron dice-game of necessity":

> Human tragedy in the *Bacchae* reminds us of its counterpart in the *Iliad*: it is the outcome of an agonistic game of wagering against infinite power, which takes either the form of the gods or, ultimately, the form of chance (tuche). Hubris is the limit or the end of the game, where chance reveals itself as necessity (ananke).[60]

Spariosu maintains that Dionysus's play is an archaic game of power, comparing it to Apollo's plotting in the *Iliad*.[61] I wish to question this critique of power. I simply doubt that a might makes right ideology is germane only to the Homeric world. Spariosu's analysis is to a certain extent presentist, insofar as he applies Enlightenment ideals to the Classical Greek period. On the other hand, it is certainly correct to assert that Euripides' *Bacchae* paints an image of the god of mask that shows him in horrific brutality.[62]

The French anthropologist René Girard gives a similar account of Dionysus in his book *La violence et le sacré* (1972). In the fifth chapter, which is simply entitled "Dionysos," he presents the god of masks and many names as an initiator of gory and cruel events. With much scrutiny Girard analyzes the climactic event, "la crise sacrificielle," in *The Bacchae* where Pentheus is the god's main antagonist, for he tries to resist Dionysian frenzy. For this reason he is slaughtered, literally ripped into pieces, by his own mother, who is temporarily blinded by Dionysus. Girard notes a play of a masked double, a monstrous double, which involves both Dionysus and Pentheus, both of whom are intermittently cast by the poet to represent the "guardian of order and tradition" and to be the enactor of transgression.[63] Girard concludes the chapter with the cynical remark: "Dionysos est le dieu du lynchage réussi."[64] Girard seems to follow Nietzsche's argument for the unity of opposites in *The Birth of Tragedy*, namely that the Dionysian is only affirmative in its interconnection with the Apollonian and totally destructive if unleashed by itself.[65] Nietzsche hails the Presocratic poets for striking a balance between the two forces—one might suggest that this is perhaps why Euripides fails, has to fail as a poet, in Nietzsche's judgment, because he simply could not grasp that kind of fine tuning, either by churning out too rationalistic plays, which are dominated by a silly question-and-answer game, nicely ridiculed in Aristophanes' *The Frogs*,[66] or by writing too chaotic, violent plays like *The Bacchae* or *The Folly of Heracles*.

While it is true that the tragic play *The Bacchae* conveys a world marred by violence and extreme disorder, I claim that it has a progressive political message: Dionysus figures as a trickster who not only ridicules the state power, namely Pentheus's absolutist authority, but also encourages women to act in defiance of the king's repressive orders. Clearly, Girard does not appreciate the notion of a "life enhancing" Dionysian frenzy and misses the subversive role this god plays in the drama. Albeit being the supreme "maître du jeu," Dionysus does not bring rules of conduct to the humans but provokes panic in those who are docile bodies—complicitous with the authoritarian state (e.g., Tiresias). In that sense I disagree with Girard's stance, according to which Dionysus merely initiates an irrational sacrificial feast for no other purpose than to demonstrate the god's own monstrosity.[67]

Euripides and Aristophanes have contrasting conceptions of life, drama, and play; Euripides stresses the Dionysian and Aristophanes the Apollonian play principle. Aristophanes merely reminisces about the past, the great Sophoclean tragic age, of not-too-human heroes. Euripides, on the other hand, uses the tragic material and gives it a new spin, e.g., in his tragedy *Medea*. In this play, he transforms the Medea of the tradition into a cunning but all-too-human mother who incites the spectator's empathy despite the transgressions she has committed. No small feat![68] For the most part, Euripides' plays lack the moralistic tone which is so prevalent in Aristophanes, who at all costs, wants to restore and preserve the Apollonian values of (social) order and beauty in a hierarchical political framework. Euripides' sociopolitical outlook clearly is more progressive, as shown by the provocative play *The Bacchae*, in which the guarantor of order, Pentheus, is mocked and a rebellion against a repressive state apparatus is encouraged.[69] Also, to write about the "banalities," the "petty amusements" of the masses, instead of the "noble" pursuits of the aristocracy, is perhaps not merely a trivial pursuit of a populist gesture.

Playful expressions vary in their mimetic representations in the Presocratic world. While both Homer and Euripides portray their respective worlds in naturalistic colors, they do not succumb to a naive, innocent perspective. Dionysian play, after all, is multifaceted; the masks (personae) of the god unleash life-affirming and life-threatening power-play. That is why both poets stand accused of using strife [*eris*] in a "bad" sense, which Hesiod, followed perhaps by Aristophanes, is trying to stamp out. Heraclitus does not quite fit into either camp. The "dark thinker" stands out in deriding the Dionysian cult and playing with god-child Dionysus at the same time. Such cunning play exemplifies his dialectical strategy of the unity of opposites—and it is this unresolved tension in his thought, the interplay of the Apollonian and Dionysian, which captivates later play theorists as diverse as Plato, Hegel, Nietzsche, and Fink.

Notes

1. Mihai Spariosu, *God of Many Names: Play, Poetry, and Power in Hellenic Thought from Homer to Aristotle* (Durham, N.C.: Duke University, 1991, henceforth "GMN"), xiii.

2. GMN, 1991, 20.

3. In the Hegelian sense of playing-alongside (*beiherspielen*), alluding to a movement of instantiation rather than to a static event.

4. "Aien aristeuein kai hypeirochon emmenai allon." See GMN for an excellent discussion of this motto.

5. GMN, 1991, 8.
6. GMN, 1991, 24.
7. GMN, 1991, 6.
8. See Günter Wohlfart, *Also sprach Herakleitos* (Freiburg: Alber, 1991), 93.
9. Schadewaldt's translation.
10. Rupé's translation, cited in Wohlfart 1991, 95.
11. It is noteworthy that play qua *athurmata* becomes early on contrasted with work.
12. GMN, 1991, 31-35.
13. I do not think that such a "median" poet as Euripides meant to portray archaic values in *Medea* and *The Bacchae* just to highlight the violence of previous eras—and to condemn it. It certainly has relevance for the bloodthirsty Pericleian age, Athens's expansionism; his plays could be taken to be a social history on his contemporary age—not of past epochs. *The Bacchae* does not display a critical and moralistic voice vis-à-vis Dionysus's behavior that a "median" poetic work ought to express. Also, despite the crimes Medea commits, Euripides is sympathetic to her plight. (See Pietro Pucci, *The Violence of Pity in Euripides' Medea* [Ithaca, N.Y.: Cornell University, 1980] and my "Mothers and Monsters" paper, unpublished ms.)
14. This move is exemplified in Spariosu's earlier work where he delineates prerational and rational ludic values and—in a seemingly Heideggerian move—suggests that Nietzsche returns to the prerational play-world of Heraclitus. See Mihai Spariosu, *Dionysus Reborn: Play and the Aesthetic Dimension in Modern Philosophical and Scientific Discourse* (Ithaca, N.Y.: Cornell University, 1989). To suggest that Platonic rational discourse is not tainted by agonistic posturing and only involves fair, nonviolent play glosses over the fact that Socrates enjoys toying with sophistry and needling his opponents with "what is F?" questions which end up leaving them perplexed and befuddled. (Cf. Gareth Matthews's discussion of aporia in his paper "Perplexity in Plato," presented at Macalester College, St. Paul, Minn., January 15, 1997.) Racing towards the better argument may not result in bodily injuries, yet it may cause humiliation, psychological distress in the losing opponent (interlocutor).
15. Erich Auerbach, *Mimesis. The Representation of Reality in Western Literature* (Princeton, N.J.: Princeton University, 1953), 13.
16. Ibid.
17. See also Hermann Fränkel's assessment of the fragility of human life in *Early Greek Poetry and Philosophy,* trans. M. Hadas and J. Willis (New York: Harcourt Brace Jovanovich, 1975).
18. Throughout the *Iliad*, young fighters hurl insults at each other on the battlefield, such as not to act like old men or women (too weak to fight) or children (ignorant of telling the difference between action and speech). On this point see W. Thomas MacCary, *Childlike Achilles. Ontogeny and Phylogeny in the* Iliad (New York: Columbia University, 1982), 212.
19. Fränkel, 1975, 54; cf. Il. 21, 389.
20. I will rely on Schadewaldt's philological analysis of the origins of the verses:
Book 1: all verses are in B
Book 6: in A
Book 8: the whole contest belongs to B
Book 17: both in A
Book 21: in A
Book 23: both in B (Homer, *Die Odyssee,* trans. W. Schadewaldt, Frankfurt: Insel, 1957), 330.
21. *Die Odyssee,* 1957, 328.
22. Cf. *Odyssey,* 1,152 with 21,430.
23. GMN, 1991, 53.

24. Johan Huizinga, *Homo Ludens* (Boston: Beacon, 1950). See my paper "Play in Culture and the Jargon of Primordiality: A Critique of Huizinga's *Homo Ludens*," in *Play and Culture Studies*, vol. 1 (Duncan et al., ed. Greenwich, Conn.: Ablex Publications, 1998).

25. What is more likely, as recent philological scholarship on Hesiod and Homer has shown, is that they draw on the same oral tradition, using a common source of formulas. Hesiod or the Hesiodic poets depend as much on the *Odyssey* as Homer/Homeric poets depend on the *Theogony* (cf. Lamberton, *Hesiod* (New Haven, Conn.: Yale University, 1988), 20.

26. Unless otherwise indicated, I use Frazer's translation, *The Poems of Hesiod*, (Norman: University of Oklahoma Press, 1983).

27. Cf. Lamberton, 1988, 58.

28. On this point, cf. Pucci, *Hesiod and the Language of Poetry* (Baltimore, Md.: Johns Hopkins, 1977), 10.

29. Pucci's translation, 1977, 9.

30. Cf. Pucci's (1977) excellent analysis of this topic in Chapter 1 "The True and False Discourse in Hesiod."

31. On "straight" and "crooked" decision see *Theog.* 85 ff.; also cf. Pucci, 1977, 16-21.

32. On this point, cf. Pucci (1977) who suggests that the Muses' logic "adds itself to things without vicariously intruding a sound or body of its own," 28.

33. Pucci (1977) notes that Hesiod is unable to "control the difference that marks his discourse." Truth and falsehood may not be that far apart (i.e., as opposites), 27.

34. Lamberton, 1988, 59.

35. Hesiod "translates" by reversing the directionality of the usual meaning: "she who has [brings] all gifts." Cf. Pucci, 1977, 97.

36. However, an incommensurable difference is that women are celebrants in the Dionysian cult and not vilified Nietzsche (1968) makes a similar point about the presence of Dionysus in Greek tragedy: "Dionysus never ceased to be the tragic hero; ... all the celebrated figures of the Greek stage—Prometheus, Oedipus, etc.—are mere masks of this original hero, Dionysus," 73.

37. Perhaps it is not farfetched to compare Hobbes's and Hesiod's conservative politics, each of them longing to preserve the old orderly monarchical ways and resenting the mayhem of wars in their respective lifetimes.

38. This "glorious" goddess is one of the few (female) deities who are deeply revered by Hesiod; it is noteworthy that Hesiod does not comment on her mischievous behavior—yet it is followed by a section that spews with anger over the mischief (mortal) women bring upon their husbands. Every misogynist theology/theogony makes allowances for one sacrosanct Woman put on a pedestal. But then again, hostility of gods towards human beings is Hesiod's main staple. On the relation of gods and men and Plato's aesthetic reappraisal/critical assessment, see Lamberton, 90-104. Particularly insightful is his discussion of the two explanatory narratives (*aitia*) dominating in *Theog.*, "why do we sacrifice as we do?" and "why is our life as miserable as it is?" Hesiod does not care where women come from (not a relevant aition) but is only concerned with their creation insofar as they explain Zeus's hostility towards men and thus man's wretched condition on earth (Lamberton, 1988), 100.

39. Cf. Spariosu's lengthy discussion of this fable (GMN, 1991), 1-49.

40. Pucci, 1977, 131.

41. I owe this point to John Brentlinger.

42. Perhaps this fragment motivated Freud to talk about a death-drive and a pleasure-drive.

43. Fränkel, 1975, 396.

44. "aion pais esti paizon, pesseuon: paidos e basilen" (B52). Diels/Kranz translate: "Das ewige Leben ist ein Kind, spielend wie ein Kind, die Brettsteine setzend; die Herrschaft gehört einem Kind."
45. Kahn's translation, *The Art and Thought of Heraclitus* (Cambridge, 1979).
46. Fink, *Spiel als Weltsymbol* (Stuttgart, 1960), 28-29.
47. Fink, 1960, 30.
48. Fränkel, 1960, 264.
49. Fränkel, 1975, 393.
50. Fränkel, 1975, 259. Wohlfart critiques the anachronism in Fränkel's analysis: he notes that it is too value-laden to declare a child as "contemptible," a better description would be "weak" or "simple minded," cf. Wohlfart, 1991, 86.
51. Fränkel, 1975, 382.
52. Wohlfart aptly summarizes the significance of the child imagery in the following: "I think that Heraclitus begins with contemporary [i.e., timely, M.N.] conceptions of the inadequacy of the child in comparison to the adult person, as is indicated in the context of his other children-fragments, but then he transcends untimely—even though not falling outside the realm of early Greek thought—this conception, because he attests that the child has more insight than the ignorant many (the adults)—who, however, are not mentioned in [fr.] 52" (1991), 93, his emphasis.
53. Kahn, 1979, 227; cf. B 30.
54. Wohlfart, 1991, 105.
55. Cf. *Laws*, 903d-e; Wohlfart, 1991, 104-7. One of Wohlfart's most devastating and brilliant critiques of interpretations of fr. B52 is directed against Heidegger, who is portrayed as one of the worst offenders of irresponsible scholarship by tailoring his account to Nazi ideology (cf. Heidegger's 1934/35 lecture, GA 39, 105; and more ominous, his 1943 lecture on Heraclitus, GA 55, 180), Wohlfart, 1991, 219-26.
56. Cf. Wohlfart, 1991, 189-96.
57. Wohlfart, 1991, 197. Also cf. Plato *Laws* 903de (on the analogy of board play and king-play): a virtuous board player distributes better lots to those characters who promise moral improvement and those who do less well to a lesser lot/place.
58. On the meaning of masks, cf. Deleuze, *Difference and Repetition*, 1994, 17.
59. This is exactly the point Nietzsche makes in "Birth of Tragedy" where he charges that Euripides brings about the death of Dionysus as tragic hero in *Basic Writings*, trans., ed., W. Kaufmann, (New York: Random House, 1968), 73. In Kaufmann's words, Euripides produces a "tragedy made lite," 77. Nietzsche thunders that "[c]ivic mediocrity was now given a voice, while heretofore the demigod in tragedy and the drunken satyr, or demiman, in comedy, had determined the character of the language," 77-78.
60. GMN, 1991, 109.
61. Cf. *Iliad* 15, 361-66 and GMN, 1991, 113.
62. It seems to me that this fascination with monstrous others finds its pendant in the modern horror film (*Friday the 13th, Texas Chainsaw Massacre, Silence of the Lambs*, etc.).
63. The double of Dionysus and Pentheus:
-Dionysos: (a) "le gardien jaloux de l'égalité, le défenseur des lois divines et humaines;" b) "subversif et dissolvant de l'action tragique."
-Pentheus: (a) "conservateur pieux, un protecteur de l'ordre traditionel;" (b) "transgresseur contribue au désordre qu'il prétend empàcher" (Girard, *La violence et le sacré*, [Paris, 1972], 182).
64. "Dionysus is the god of successful lynching," Girard 1972, 190.
65. On this point, cf. Ackermann, 1990 (passim).
66. Particularly dull in that way is Euripides' *The Cyclops*.

67. Feminists have noted the subversive political meanings of Euripides' work. Froma Zeitlin notes: ". . . Euripides may be said to have 'feminized' tragedy and, like his Dionysos in the *Bakkhai*, to have laid himself open to the scorn that accrues to those men who consort with women. Aristophanic comedy, which loves to lampoon Euripides and all his newfangled ideas, continually presses the scandal of his erotic dramas, especially those that let women speak more boldly (and hence more shamefully) on the stage" ("Playing the Other," in *Representations II* [1985]: 88).

68. Cf. my "Mothers and Monsters" paper (unpublished ms.).

69. This is indeed an interpretation put forth by Nigerian playwright Wole Soyinka in his version of the *Bacchae* (*The Bacchae of Euripides: A Communion Rite*. New York: Norton, 1975).

Chapter 2

PLATO'S PLAY: THE DEMISE OF THE DIONYSIAN?

Most thinkers who seek out favorable uses of play in philosophical thought tend to dismiss Plato's engagement with play as a rationalistic reduction, as an abstract negation or "spirit murder" of Dionysus. Philosophical discourse is not only utterly demystified but what remains—at best—is an abstract, monological play of the philosopher with himself.[1] According to this view, a Heraclitean, life-affirming play of the opposites completely vanishes from the Platonic horizon. Poetry and rhetoric are played out against philosophy, because they lack techne and seriousness.[2] Thus elevated as superior techne, philosophy is cast as being void of playful trickery and Plato stands accused of initiating a "repression of play."[3] This harsh critique seems justified in light of Plato's indictment of certain kinds of poetic representations as being far removed from the Ideal, from Truth, and as rendering heroic (male) actions as effeminate; hence Plato also is guilty of initiating the erasure of female mimetic play.[4]

Yet, it remains to be seen that Plato is indeed the *enfant terrible* who eradicates the promises of Dionysian playfulness in philosophical discourse. Plato asks about what counts as good play, about the value of child's play, and whether philosophers should be allowed to be playful. To be sure, in the notorious critique of the poets in the *Republic*, play (*paidia*) is associated with mimesis, which is the art, or rather pseudo-art, of the poets. Furthermore, play qua child's play seems to be contrasted with seriousness, supposedly the activity of an adult. Both connotations suggest a devaluation of playful activities—unworthy of a philosopher's participation. However, this reading of Plato's argument is reductivistic. The uses of play (*paidia*) in the dialogues are varied: undeniably, jest, mimicry, and mockery spice Socrates' elenctic method, which is designed to drive his opponents into surrendering their positions. Playful irony is an important stylistic tool of the Socratic discourse, as revealed by his student Alcibiades in the *Symposium*. More often than not, play is conjoined with seriousness, as illustrated in the *Euthydemus*, *Phaedrus*, and even the *Laws*. Playful seriousness and serious play are important ingredients of dialectics—to be neither sacrificed nor maligned (or, if so, only in jest) in the Platonic dialogue.[5] After all, he tends to appropriate play in various ways, ranging from advocating the usefulness of play in moral education (by provoking perplexity), of pretend-play, toying with the sophists (e.g., by challenging simplistic assumptions), of play in myth-telling, to denouncing irresponsible mimesis. Plato's writings indicate an ambivalent attitude towards play: on the one hand, playfulness seems to suffer in comparison to reason and seriousness and, on the other, its status is elevated by being the divine in human beings. A more accurate and complex reading discloses the following in the Platonic view of play: (a) an ontological malediction of (mere) play and benediction of seriousness (e.g., in the *Republic*); (b) an ethical polarization of "good" and "bad" play (e.g., in *Phaedrus*); and (c) an ontological benediction of play ("as being the best in humans" *Laws* 803c-d). In addition, I will examine the rhetorical and stylistic devices Socrates employs, to show how he elucidates play—and eludes play by donning "serious" masks.

The Masking of Truth: Plato's Play with Mimesis in the *Republic*

In the *Republic*, Plato gives an indirect account of *paidia*'s ontological ranking by maligning the uses of mimesis in his famous critique of the poets as exemplified in his accounts of mimesis in Book III and Book X.[6]

In Book III Plato imposes a series of guidelines as to what counts as permissible mimetic representations of human heroism in the best state. First, he calls for a reform of poetic narratives. Homer is rebuked for relying extensively on mimetic—and hence dramatic—representation in his *epos*: his narrator impersonates[7] the hero by using direct speech (III.393ab). Homer fails to exercise good judgment because he does not employ the proper mix of narration (indirect speech) and mimesis (direct speech). According to Plato, impersonation should only be "a small part of a long tale"[8] and should avoid mimicking ludicrous or banal things, such as "thunder and the noise of wind and of hail, of axles and of wheels, of trumpets and flutes and pipes . . . the cries of dogs and sheep and birds" (III.396e-97a). A properly playful representation is one in which the emotions do not interfere with the cognitive faculties of the listener. Hence, deceptive play, which merely appeals to feelings of pleasure (and pain), is ruled out. By restricting the use of direct speech, the emotional spell which the minstrel casts over his captive audience is undermined so that narration creates a critical distance (of the viewer/listener) to the enacted plot. The spectator may be less tempted to identify with the emotions of the hero.[9]

Second, Plato introduces a normative polarization of playfulness and seriousness. Mimesis is permissible if the actions of a good person (*agathos*) are impersonated (*Rep.* III.396d). Plato also advises against a *serious* imitation of bad actions or persons, since they might lead one astray to taste—and enjoy!—being a bad character, thus the actor might be tempted to become that *persona* (mask) which he impersonates (III.395c 7). Interestingly, it is possible to imitate bad actions; yet it may only be done *in jest*, i.e., a comic mockery, in order to maintain the critical (serious) distance between playing the morally reprehensible person and being seduced into adopting his character flaws (396e). It thus becomes clear why Plato singles out the tragedians in his attack, since tragic art does not allow for such buffoonery—even the wicked have to be portrayed in earnest. Plato seems worried that artists are susceptible to assuming the mis-guided ideals that they embody on stage.

While Plato focuses mostly on the impersonating aspects of mimesis in Book III, he looks at mimesis as imitation in Book X. It is in this last Book of the *Republic*, which is often regarded as a supplement, rather than an integral part of the core argumentation of his vision of the best state, where Plato launches his famous attack on mimetic representation (X.595a-608b). In comparing the on-tological status of the Form (*eidos*) of a bed with the empirical object of a bed and the imitation of a bed (e.g., in a painting), the imitation is considered being at three removes from nature (or truth). The maker (*poetes*) of an artwork un-knowingly produces phantasmatic pictures of reality (e.g., in scene paintings) by falling prey to optical illusions (X.602d). The painter is faulted for not listening to the rational part of his soul; his imitation becomes psychologically suspect for being "an inferior thing and consorting with an inferior part [of the soul]" (X.603b). While Plato's Socrates begins his ontological malediction with the work of the painter, his criticism is actually foremost directed against a *poetes* of a different sort, namely the tragic poet—already maligned in Book III. The tra-gedian engages in imitation as a kind of amusement (*einai paidian tina*) which is not to be taken seriously (*Rep.* X.602b). Plato links mimesis with (mere) play and contrasts play with seriousness. He discredits the poet's truth claim by al-leging that as a mere imitator he does not have any valuable knowledge of the subject that he writes about—and worse, that he merely caters opportunistically to the taste and pleasures of the masses (X.602ab; cf. *Gorgias* 501d ff.). In this context, Plato's indictment of mimesis signals an ontologic-epistemological malediction of play, because it *is* an inferior kind of activity and it is not a guar-antor of proper validity claims. It follows from Plato's argumentation that the imitator is not a *spoudaios* (a serious, virtuous person), since "he does not know whether a particular subject is good or bad" (X.602b1-2). Unable to make such epistemic distinctions with his pseudo techne, the artist's ability to make ethical judgments (e.g., what virtues to teach Athen's youth) is also cast into doubt. So in a quite heavy-handed manner, Plato issues an ethical polarization of play ver-sus seriousness.

Plato's disparaging remarks of mimesis and poets in Book X is only miti-gated by his apologetic gesture at the end of the mimesis discussion: Plato as-certains the possibility that a certain kind of poetry, which proves itself to be a positive art form, does not need to be banished from the city. Above all, Plato's Socrates informs his interlocutor—certainly in jest—that he "does not want to be accused of a certain harshness and boorishness," since he knows very well that poetry is able to spice up the lives of the many (X.607b). Thus Plato almost seems ready to take back his earlier indictment, yet he remains firm in his (pre)judgment that poetry is neither serious nor truthful. This Platonic jest/gesture, according to Deleuze, hides behind an *ironic* mask, distinct from a *humorous* one that plays with the differences.[10]

Next, let's turn to the phenomenological critiques of Plato's interpretation of mimesis and play in Book X. Eugen Fink provides an extensive critique of the Platonic interpretation of mimesis and the mirror-model, accusing Plato of being the key culprit in the devaluation and demise of play in philosophy.[11] In Platonic thought, play is demystified when it is defined as mimesis. It loses its mythical-tragical understanding of cosmos, which is prevalent in Heraclitus.[12] Also, Fink charges that Plato simply gets the analogy wrong with his mirror-imagery:

> The play of humans is not imitated passively; it does not merely repeat mimetically an original. Strictly speaking, there is no mirroring [*Spiegelung*] in play.[13]

Fink recognizes that there is an element of playfulness in Socratic irony, but he argues that Plato is overcome by the preoccupation with putting the poets in their place and denying them any *Anspruch* (claim) to truth.[14]

Fink's scathing critique of Plato's denunciation of poetry and of play's being a mere shadow of the original (form), dismisses the Platonic jester too quickly. Plato's labelling of mimesis as "a kind of play" does not necessarily mean that play also has to be completely disavowed. Playing games for amusement's sake has its appropriate time (*kairos*).[15]

In his *Polis und Poesis*, Dalfen reevaluates Plato's conception of the poet's use of mimesis, contrasting the argumentation of the middle dialogues (e.g., *Republic*) with that of the *Laws*. Dalfen's analysis is a marked departure from Fink's dismissal of Platonic mimesis, in part because Dalfen sheds light on the sociopolitical context in which Plato was writing. He notes that Plato clashes with the sophists over the issue of whether poetry ought to give pleasure or utility (*hedone* vs. *terpsis*; cf. *Gorgias* 501d ff.; *Rep.* III). The aim of common or traditional poetry is to please the audience even if it has to offer that which is morally reprehensible. (*Gorg.* 501d); thus poets pander to the passions and pathological wishes of an audience that resents hearing that which is useful (because it's not pleasurable). In the *Laws*, Plato allows room for pleasure as long as it is enjoyable to the virtuous person, the philosophical critic, who alone judges the work of art and gives guidelines to the poets, so that they create works of art that are educational and pleasing. However, the audience's tastes have been corrupted by traditional poetry and, therefore, they have to be re-educated. Dalfen speculates that Plato criticizes his fellow citizens for their subjective decisions with respect to political trials where the jury refuses to make rationally binding judgments and favors those that it finds pleasurable.[16] For Plato, true mimesis has to be linked with *charis* (joy, charm), not *hedone*.[17] Thus transformed, *mimesis* is philosophical, i.e., knowledge-producing, unlike the deceiving, pseudo-techne mimetic works of art. In this educational game, the young citizen is supposed to be in awe of philosophical poetry and at the same time be able to learn to overcome lowly feelings of pleasure. Plato clearly wants to force a separation between the manic, persuasive power of rhetoric and crude hedonistic enjoyment.

Perhaps we can regard the example of the mirror and the painter as a *paignion* (plaything)—and even as paradigmatic model—which Plato uses in order to test the limits of knowledge about the world of appearances. Note the comic description of the painter's use of a mirror to go around and copy things quickly—and not surprisingly, the artist's work turns out to be a mirage.[18] Similarly, the tragic dramaturgist is guilty of such phantasmatic, illusory production. The comedian, however, "knows" better and is exempted from Plato's critique![19] Also, I wish to take seriously the oddity of introducing a god who creates the Real, the Form. Perhaps, god is invoked as a jester, who toys with seriousness. After all, nowhere else in Plato's writing are Forms described as being divine creations.[20] In a similarly speculative vein, one might want to reject taking the indictment of mimesis at face value and instead interpret it as a provocative gesture. How can poetry possibly be three times removed from the truth? This seems bizarre, given Plato's point about the possibility of divine inspirations experienced by poets (cf. *Ion*). Socrates' mockery plays games with our imagination and leaves us perplexed.[21]

Clearly, Plato's (and Socrates') playful masquerade also involves laughter. As William Desmond suggests, Plato highlights the mockery of philosophers in the tale of the Tracian maid in *Theaetetus* (174a). The maid's laughter, her mockery of the great philosopher (Thales), has to be taken seriously and haunts philosophical thinking to this day.[22] Riddles and jokes, as some Platonic scholars have observed, play a key role in conveying Socrates' thought, and they should not be dismissed as mere "by-play" (or *Beispiel*). Plato stays here in the tradition of the "enigmatic" philosopher due to his casting of Socrates as playful, mocking and elusive, because—much to our irritation—he evades our cognitive grasp, our *Zugriff*.

The Play of Logos/Mythos in the *Phaedrus* and *Symposium*

One may ask: Is it important for play to be handled in the right way? The *Symposium* and *Phaedrus* offer an interplay of myth and reason in such a way that they engender possibilities of Dionysian frenzy. Wendy Brown—who is sympathetic to a reevaluation of Plato's play with myths and similes—argues that we should take seriously the female personification of truth and philosophy in Plato. One ought to go beyond Nietzsche's and Derrida's charge of logocentrism and interrogate the relation of philosophy to power in Platonic writings. Socrates often finds himself mocked by the sophists, in particular by Thrasymachus who calls him a wimp for opposing the sophist's agonistic theory of power.[23] However, Brown makes no mention of the fact that Thrasymachus gets a thrashing too.[24]

Some feminists have also interpreted Plato's game as subversive in two important ways: (a) for recasting the philosophical enterprise as female—because Plato attacks the male aspects of sophistic dialectics, its agonistic mode;[25] (b) for reversing gendered roles, e.g., in Socrates' myth of love in the *Symposium*. Truth is a woman (Diotima) who plays sensuously with her lover (of wisdom).[26]

While Socrates mythologizes Diotima[27] in his speech on the nature of love and absorbs her teachings, Alcibiades puts forth his own mythic account of the historic Socrates. He employs similes to expose Socrates' method of playing in his laudatory speech (*Sym.* 215a-22c), which at the same time serves as an indictment of his teacher's cunning and "outrageous" mockery:

> To praise Socrates, gentlemen, I shall proceed as follows: through similes. He will assume that I'm ridiculing him. But the simile will be for the sake of the truth, not for ridicule. I assert he is most like the Sileni which sit in statuaries' shops—the ones which the craftsmen carve to hold shepherd's pipes or flutes, which when they are opened into two, turn out to have images of the gods inside. And I shall compare him, too, with the satyr Marsyas. (*Sym.* 215a-b)

He goes on to explain the effects of the satyr's piping on him, adding that he felt both mesmerized and intimidated by the force of Socrates' speech which uncovers Alcibiades' own moral and intellectual defects. Another posture of Silenus is to feign ignorance but when his inner self is exposed—stripped from postures and hideous masks—he is revealed as "divine, all-golden, exquisite and miraculous." Because of Silenus's superhuman and seductive powers, an enraptured Alcibiades just complies with whatever Silenus demands of him, as if they were partaking in the Bacchanalian mysteries (cf. *Sym.* 217a).

In the end of his bombastic speech, Alcibiades unravels the meaning of the similes of Sileni and Satyrs. Upon opening up the Sileni, one discovers that what at first glance is ridiculous and obscene—as satyrs commonly are depicted—is serious stuff, which is only revealed through a hermeneutic engagement with the matter:

> His arguments are all clothed by words and phrases which are like the hide of an impudent Satyr, for he speaks of millstones and pack-asses, of smithies, shoemaker's shops and tanners, and through all these things seems to be repeating himself over and over, so that any ignorant fool would laugh at the things he says. But if one sees them opened up and penetrates into them, one finds to begin with that they are the only discourses [*logoi*] that make any sense; and later that they have a great divinity, that they are filled with the images of virtue, in themselves, and when they are extended to their fullest meaning they encompass everything that it becomes a man to contemplate who is seeking to achieve the beautiful and the good. (*Sym.* 221e-222a)

Alcibiades's play with satyr/silenus similes alludes to a god who is often mistakenly represented as a laughingstock by the uninitiated—Dionysus, the god of many names. It has been argued that the entire dramatic action of the *Symposium* mirrors the series of events of the Dionysian cult in a four-day span.[28] According to John Brentlinger, it begins with Agathon's victory at a festival celebrating Dionysus's birth followed by a day of sacrifice in honor of the god, which involves heavy drinking. On the third day, Agathon's friends congregate in his house, where they have a contest as to who can give a superior speech on love, and finally succumb to a deep sleep or Bacchanalian revel, except for Socrates, who, as Brentlinger puts it suggestively, "rising to begin the fourth day with a bath at the Lyceum, is like a risen god among the debris of spent mortality. He, it appears, and not Agathon, is the victor and the true symbol of Dionysus."[29]

Yet this apparently sober god dons grotesque masks: Sileni or satyrs are sexually charged monsters, who are frequently depicted as being hunched over (like servants!) in order to masturbate to oblivion.[30] This peculiar game of the mask-bearer (Silenus), which combines elements of selfconscious cleverness and uncontrollable, divine inspiration, is played out in Socrates' conflation of myth and logos. After all, the true philosopher is—according to the description of the *Phaedrus*—"out of his wits" and "overcome by divine madness" (cf. also *Ion*). Yet, even when overcome in this precarious way, Plato's make-belief play differentiates carefully between the mad philosopher and mere poetic madness, insofar as he is sober enough to not completely lose his grip over logos. In his play with seriousness, Socrates sends away the flute players in order to provide for his fellow symposium revelers in a different kind of entertainment. But logos runs away from Plato's spin. Suffice it to say that Dionysian frenzy—even where tempered with Apollonian order—is an integral part of Platonic dialectic but has been overlooked for the most part by twentieth-century Plato scholarship, which has been partial to Nietzsche's indictment of Socrates as being responsible for entombing the archaic logos. We should distinguish between an author's intentions, which we cannot authenticate, and the impact of Socratic speech on his audience, which leaves them truly mesmerized—even despite the author's intentions. Plato may intend to control Dionysus, but he fails to perform this stricture.

Where Dionysian masquerade is foregrounded in the *Symposium*, myths play an important role in the *Phaedrus*. Elias's book *Plato's Defense of the Poets* (1984) argues that we should reevaluate Plato's scathing attacks on the poets by considering the function and role of the myths in Plato's dialectics. Elias gives a "strong defense" of poetry, since myths play an essential role in Platonic thought and are invoked where dialectic fails to prove first premises.[31] Elias's point that we should take the myths more seriously is well taken. Plato does not simply employ functional arguments when he uses myths as ammunition for endorsing the dialogical method. To be sure, while myths are seriously reckoned with and employed by Socrates, we still have to deal with Plato's famous challenge that if mimetic poetry is to show a reason for her existence, she needs to provide a benefit other than pleasure (cf. *Republic* X.607cd). So, Deleuze, for example, counters Elias's strong defense that far from expelling poetry and myths from his city, Plato retools myths and fits them neatly into his dialectic.[32] Let's turn to the *Phaedrus* to assess Deleuze's criticism.

The *Phaedrus* displays Plato's strategic use of myths.[33] In the opening scene, Socrates ridicules a sophistic interpretation of a myth and claims that he is generally not interested in bothering with mythologemes; he is just as happy to leave these *logoi* to the sophists (*Phaedr.* 229c-30a). However, this emphatic disavowal of myths has an ambiguous meaning, as Derrida notes in his article "Plato's Pharmacy": "bidding myths a farewell" also suggests a salute.[34] Throughout the dialogue Socrates plays with the opposites of giving a rational account (logos) and merely telling a story (mythos), suggesting that he is not seriously advocating a dismissal of mythologemes and that it seems implausible to try to force a rationalistic division between the two concepts.[35]

In fact, later in the discussion of what constitutes good writing, Plato introduces two original myths[36] as *logoi*: the fable of the cicadas (259b3-59d9) and the story of Theuth (274b9-75c4).[37] I will focus on the latter, since it is part of an argument which introduces *paidia*. In this myth, Theuth presents the letters as a *pharmakon* (a remedy, drug, or poison) to King Thamus of Egypt. The king, however, immediately rejects the gift,[38] pointing to its toxic rather than beneficial effects; writing after all makes people forgetful, since they don't have to rely on the power of remembrance. Plato here uses Theuth as a divine trickster—note that Socrates is often cast as magician[39]—who, according to Derrida, distributes his *pharmakai* carelessly and callously: "[Theuth] cannot be assigned a fixed spot in the play of differences. Sly, slippery, and masked, an intriguer and a card, like Hermes, he is neither king nor jack, but rather a sort of *joker*, a floating signifier, a wild card, one who puts play into play."[40] "Putting play into play" is Derrida's shrewd observation that in his myth, Socrates attributes the invention of games (draughts and dice) to Theuth (274d), who tricks the king into giving his stamp of approval for such frivolous matters. The invocation of games seems to be an anticipation of the play writings of the dialectician (276b ff).

Analogous to the playful conflation of the mythos/logos dichotomy discussed above, Plato conjoins play with seriousness when it comes to philosophical writings/musings. The unity of this oppositional couple is featured in the following passage, where Socrates poses these questions to Phaedrus:

> And tell me this. Would a sensible farmer, who cared about his seeds and wanted them to yield fruit, plant them in all seriousness in the gardens of Adonis in the middle of the summer and enjoy watching them bear fruit within seven days? Or would he do this as an amusement and in honor of the holiday, if he did it at all? Wouldn't he use his knowledge of farming to plant the seeds he cared for when it was appropriate and be content if they bore fruit seven months later? (276b-c, trans. Nehemas and Woodruff)

Phaedrus agrees that a serious farmer would not force a harvest as is done with the pot plants that bear fruit during the festival of Adonis.[41] The practices of the insincere farmer are criticized—Socrates' swipe against the sophists who pride themselves on teaching their methods quickly.[42] The dialectician (not unlike a Demiurge) earnestly and in a leisurely manner selects a proper soul in order to implant it with the seeds of logos and to recognize that it takes time for this to take fruition in the form of self-knowledge (276e-77a). While the amusement in the gardens of Adonis may not be the sort of game the true philosopher indulges in and condones, we have to make note of the irony in the comparison of writing with painting which precedes the agricultural trope. Socrates warns that "writing shares a strange [*schlimme*; trans. Schleiermacher] feature with painting. The offsprings of painting stand there as if they are alive, but if anyone asks them anything they remain most solemnly silent. The same is true of written words." (275d; trans. Nehemas and Woodruff). If *Mimesisverbot* extends to writing, it has grave consequences for Plato's (written) work, which cannot just pretend to engage in and sustain itself in living dialogue. Plato stands accused of reinscribing *doxosophia* and not genuine knowledge. Plato is aware of such pitfalls and, rather than disavowing or feigning to disavow imitation (in print), he is not really interested in advocating an absolute prohibition of mimesis nor, for that matter, of myths.

Furthermore, the allegory of writing as a play of the dialectician illustrates the mixing of play and seriousness. However, it maintains and reinforces a division of lesser and nobler kinds of games; that is, a polarization of play in the good and bad sense, weeding out false fruit, i.e., drinking parties and other base amusements (276d), from good fruit, such as philosophical conversations (276e).[43]

To a certain extent, Plato's *Symposium* and *Phaedrus* seem to rehabilitate the notion of play and myths. Yet, in his pursuit of the true art of philosophizing, that is, dialectically, Plato imposes a standard of what constitutes superior play. Nevertheless, Wendy Brown encourages an oppositional reading, suggesting that we ought to realize that Dionysian *paidia* is also immanent in Platonic philosophy and that Plato is as a poet "the celebrant of eros, the dreamer, the maker of myths and allegories."[44] Recognizing Plato's flirtation with the Dionysian, Brown claims that Plato's Socrates does not provide a theory of knowledge that is void of sensuousness, madness, and playfulness. Singling out one passage in the *Republic* (481d-82d), she comments: "Socrates develops the image of the passionately sexual, monogamous, possessive, and creative lover of wisdom in a passage that moves from the sexual act to procreation and birth in a split second."[45] Taking a cue from Brown's irreverent reading of Platonic truth, rather than quibbling over where myth differs from truth-telling *logoi*, one should simply note that when Plato wants to give us a "true story" he reverts to myth-making, which is his play with seriousness.[46]

Agonistic Play in the Dialogues

The *Euthydemus* is paradigmatic for Socrates' display for agonism: taking on the sophists by engaging in their eristic game. In this dialogue, Plato exposes the fallacy of the sophist's claim that false speaking and teaching (virtue) are compatible with each other. In Socrates' vigorous pursuit of this argument, it becomes apparent that agonistic play is just as much a feature of Platonic philosophy as it is of sophistic thought.

Many Plato scholars have commented on the use of irony in Socrates' philosophical dialogues. I hold that irony, in Plato's idiosyncratic casting of it, namely in the interplay of jest and seriousness, plays an important part in his style; it does not simply serve an instrumental function, illustrating the sophist's game satirically. On the other hand, Spariosu (1991) and Wendy Brown (1994) both contend that play as agon merely portrays Socrates' verbal contest with cantankerous sophists to beat them at their own game. Yet, all of the dialogues of the middle period are driven by an agonistic, ironic modus operandi. It is not something that Plato gives up even when he has Socrates converse with the youth or his adult friends.

Similarly, Friedländer (1954) argues that play is a feature of Socrates' posture, but it is a peculiar play, namely of irony (of hiding something, a game of skillful deception while at the same time stating the truth, without polite reservations).[47] Friedländer states that one of the richest examples of "ironic polyphony" can be found in the *Euthydemus*. In this dialogue, the sophists perform a great "firework of the most bombastic eristic artistry" only to be beaten by Socrates' simple ironic stance. But his ironic tone takes on different tunes; it oscillates between a grimacing one and a relaxed sotto voce.[48] I would however claim that Socrates is not too comfortable in the role of a soothsayer—although Plato tries hard not to let Socrates' ironic attitude overpower the dialogue and occasionally lets him come to Cleinias's or Ctesippus's rescue, where they falter in answering the sophists' trick questions.

Socrates mocks the sophists by using the dichotomy of play and seriousness ironically: Encouraging Cleinias not to be intimidated by their sheer overpowering argumentation and trick questions and insisting that they have in fact failed to teach him anything useful with their superficial play, Socrates bursts out into this tirade: "So you must think of their performance as having been mere play. But after this they will doubtless show you serious things, if anyone will, and I shall give them a lead to make sure they hand over what they promised me. . . . So, Euthydemus and Dionysodorus, put an end to this joking"(278c-d; trans. Sprague).

With this stern speech Socrates promises to fight it out with the sophists. This competitive game turns out to be harder than he first thought: Socrates confesses to his friend Crito that he has lost round one by being thrown into a state of perplexity[49] and being duped by Dionysodorus, who claims that to wish that somebody becomes wise, who is not, means to wish for nothing else but his death (*Euth.* 283d). Socrates, however, recovers from this defeat and gains the upper hand by focusing on the misuses of reason; he does this—in typically ironic manner—by misleading the sophist with phrases, such as "I am rather thickwitted and don't understand these fine clever things" (286e). Moreover, Socrates spoils the game by provoking the sophist with counterquestions, e.g., in Euthydemus's proof that Socrates always already knows everything (295b-d). In the end, Socrates seems to succumb to the eristic game; however, the sophists' triumph is ridiculed by Plato, who attributes the following imbecilic question to a jubilant Dionysodorus: "Is Heracles a bravo, or is a bravo Heracles?" (303a).[50] Socrates, however, has the last laugh, telling the sophists that the rules for their game are easily learnt (303e) and, in an ironic voice, advises them to keep their game to themselves lest they want to forgo remuneration for teaching their art to the crowd (303e-4b).

While Socrates excels in eristic art, he advocates a superior techne, namely dialectics, hardly a "worthless affair and chattering" (cf. 305e); nevertheless Plato is ambivalent about discarding the sophistic eris. That is why I argue against Spariosu, who holds that agonism (and by extension, Dionysian tragic art) is eclipsed in Platonic dialectics and a median, nonviolent, cooperative (Apollonian) spirit of rationality ushered in. Socrates may appear to dispute less aggressively with inexperienced interlocutors (e.g., Charmides), but he argues no less vigorously than the sophists. A spirit of defiance, i.e., an unwillingness to end disputes in a draw, often marks the end of a dialogue; at the same time Socrates wears his comic mask, embodying Dionysian buffoonery, which seems especially untimely when serious ethical matters are to be discussed.[51] For example, in the final passages of the *Gorgias* Socrates practically gives a soliloquy, because Callicles is too annoyed to answer the impertinent questioner on the nature of temperance. Callicles brushes off Socrates, suggesting that he carry on the dialogue with somebody else (505c), while Socrates pretends to be insulted ("Well, but people say that a tale cannot rightly be left half-finished; a head must be put on it, that it may not run about headless."[52]) and forces Callicles to continue his role as an interlocutor. The sophist begins to agree with every point made by Socrates in order to hasten the end of the speech ("Granted, Socrates, in order that you may bring your argument to an end" 510a).

Another case in point is the final scene of the *Symposium*: as Agathon and Alcibiades are falling asleep, a sober Socrates carries on the conversation and coerces them to accept his viewpoint. According to Aristodemus's account, he tells them "that it was possible for the same man to know how to write comedy and tragedy, and that the skilled tragedian can write comedy as well. Well, they were being forced to agree to all this, but they weren't following it very actively, and were dozing off"(*Sym.* 223d).Yet, does this mean that Socrates is so sober as to lose his playful ironic stance? Even if it appears that Dionysus has no grip over his ability to carry on lucid conversations, this may just be part of his satyr/satiric repertoire.

Another example which displays Socrates' eristic bravura occurs in the *Ion* where he mocks the rhapsode for claiming that his art enables him to be a good general as well and that such art must rely on divine inspiration.

Socrates' irony is also manifest in his pretend-play, hereby mocking the interlocutor, or the audience, taking on different roles, befitting a satyr. For instance, in the aporetic dialogue, *Charmides*, Socrates asks the adolescent man what he makes of temperance (*ti esti sophrosyne*). Charmides stumbles to give a reasonable definition, which eventually leads nowhere, guided by the probing questions of his thoughtful mentor and teacher. At the same time, Socrates pretends to be virtually overcome by his own "intemperance," i.e., his sexual attraction towards Charmides, thus mocking the bystanders who are literally in awe of the adolescent's strikingly good looks.

Clearly the deceptive mask of a satyr is important for this game, that is hiding a fierceful soul behind a smiling and grotesque facade. Socrates' game is about winning an argument—prevailing in the name of truth. It has defined the way we conduct the "business" of philosophizing, and only recently this agonistic game has come under criticism by feminists who seek to introduce playfulness as "loving perception."[53]

Irony secedes perhaps—as suggested by Dalfen (1974)—in the later dialogues. In his esoteric works, which are not intended for the public eye, Plato does not see the need for ironic attacks of the sophists, e.g., he reinscribes positively the manic-mantic connection in the philosopher (cf. *Phaedrus*), and it is in dialogues, such as the *Laws* and *Timaeus*, where he inscribes a benediction of play and revisits the meaning of mimesis. The philosopher's business is the highest among the arts (*musike*) as indicated already in *Phaidon* (61a); he is the true poet whose tragic plays imitate the true and best life (*Laws* 817b).[54] Poetic mimesis plays a new role as philosophical mimesis.

Many passages in Plato's dialogues are inherently playful (in the sense of donning cunning or mocking roles and of being a cooperative, good sport). Nevertheless, he clearly sets up a game of a polarization between good and bad play as Spariosu (1991) and Derrida (1981) suggest. However, I believe Spariosu (following Nietzsche) goes too far in stating that Plato banishes the archaic or prerational forms of play (e.g., agonistic, eristic) and introduces median or rational (cooperative) aspects (e.g., in the contest between the poet and philosopher in Book X of the *Republic*).[55] To be sure, Plato is intent on differentiating philosophical inspiration or madness from a mere poetic one, and is particularly intent on lashing out at the sophists for feigning truthful discourse. Yet, it is a misrepresentation of Plato's thought to state there are prohibitions against archaic, agonistic, and mimetic expressions of play.

Plato's early dialogues are highly competitive in their nature, perhaps because they were performed at the Olympic games. Here, Socrates, as interlocutor, comes across as a spoilsport, a cunning manipulator, a trickster, and a fighter, by harping on the elenctic method. As Ryle (1966) explains, the purpose of this method is to drive "interlocutors by sequences of questions into admitting falsity of theses that they have been defending."[56] Rather than admitting to a self-serving double standard—Plato denounces cunning poets (in the third book of the *Republic*) and advocates that they be thrown out of the city—he insists that the elenctic dialogue has a pedagogic function, but dialectics should not be used for the education of young men. If they had a taste of the art of dialectics, Plato cautions:

> they take it as a game and always use it to contradict. They imitate those who cross-examined them and themselves cross-examine others, rejoicing like puppies to drag alcng and tear to bits in argument whoever is near them.—Yes, to excess. And when they have themselves cross-examined many people and been cross-examined by many, they fall vehemently and quickly into disbelieving what they believed before. As a result, they themselves, and the whole of philosophy are discredited in the eyes of other men.—Very true. (VII.539bc)

Such "playing and contradicting for play" mocks the serious business of philosophizing and drags it down to the level of a farce. Philosophical discourse cannot tolerate such a delegitimizing act and needs to send away taunting adolescent boys and female flute players. The playful exposé of the failure of the logos has to be cast as an act of sacrilege. Play is thus cast as the Other of Reason. However, for Plato, other forms of play have legitimacy, as long as they are enacted seriously. As pointed out by Wendy Brown (1994), what is unusual about the dialogical form is that Socrates changes his forms of attack, whether it is to match the style of the agonistic opponent he sees in Thrasymachus or Gorgias or whether to accomodate timid, less sophisticated companions such as Charmides or Glaukon. Brown claims that competitiveness is not an end in itself for Socrates, who attacks the sophists for their eristic dialectical practice, but it is something he performs *con gusto*.

Clearly, agonistic, mocking play displays Socrates' Dionysian masquerade, which is juxtaposed to an Apollonian imposition of a hierarchical ranking of play; both frenzied and orderly expressions of play coexist uneasily and contribute to the semiotic indeterminacy which is symbolized as a *pharmakon*, a gift of Dionysos—one is never quite sure whether taking the potion is life-affirming or whether it is deadly and its toxic effects strike the player, gradually numbing her limbs.

Playfulness as an Existentiale in the *Laws*

The *Laws* are relevant to our discussion of Plato's play theory insofar as they address the issue of what is the "best" play. Also, this dialogue provides a clue as to how Plato ranks play with respect to other human activities, and with respect to how his views turn out to be when he revisits the dichotomy between play and seriousness. While the *Laws* have been described as a "non-agonistic dialogue,"[57] which is certainly true in terms of the style of the conversation, I want to maintain that, with respect to the content, Plato weighs both sides of Hesiod's *eris*, that is peaceful, nonlethal strife vs. warrior strife, and ends up privileging the former. In other words, Dionysian excess is tamed by Apollonian harmony and order, especially in the case of regulating wine consumption at symposia and Bacchanalian revelry (cf. 653d, 654a; 666b; 671a-d). Yet this does not mean that *agon* (contest) simply gets discarded.

In the so called theologia ludens passage[58] of Book VII, where the Demiurge figures as puppeteer, thus reiterating the *paignon* theme hypothesized in Book I (654d), Plato makes a stronger claim by arguing that in fact the human being "is made to be the plaything of God, and that this, truly considered, is the best of him; wherefore every man and every woman should follow in this way, and pass life in the noblest of pastimes, be of another mind from what they now are" (803c-d). This other—deviant—perspective is the pursuit of a life of peace which includes participating in sacrificial games, singing, and dancing, rather than a life of a warrior (804d-e). This novel approach resonates with the one put forth by Hesiod in his famous hawk/nightingale simile.[59] However, unlike the scornful Hesiodic poet, Plato does not sanction a particular kind of play which is truly cooperative. It is difficult to imagine that his Stranger would voice a prohibition against *agon*.

What is interesting about Plato's proposal is that he sheds new light on the as-if approach of play,[60] he prefaces his theophilia play account with the statement that seriousness in this context is being toyed with for its own sake (or perhaps for assuring our sanity as mortals). After all, "human affairs are hardly worth considering in earnest, and yet we must be in earnest" (803b). This point is emphasized again at the end of the simile that the pupils should just carry on with their delightful games to please the gods, but *we* should realize that they are "for the most part puppets, but having some little share of reality" (804b). Tasting a part of Being, of Truth is a divine affair (cf. *Rep.* III.395c). However, Plato's extreme view is rebuked by Megillus: "you have a low opinion of mankind, Stranger" (804b). To which Plato's Stranger responds kindly, " . . . And let us grant, if you wish, that the human race is not to be despised, but is worthy of some consideration" (804b-c). In this ironic manner, he again dangles the oppositional pair, play and seriousness, in front of the interlocutor.

Finally, I want to mention a different account of play, which Plato puts forth as a straw man argument for elevating another aspect of his play theory. This concerns Plato's critique of atheists (X.888e), who, he says, believe that *phusis* and *tuche* produce the best values of the world, not god. Techne (art) which comes later into existence produces mere games (*paidias tinas*) that only mimic truth; however arts in connection with natural sciences produce serious things (X.889c-d). Thus, play, being removed from *phusis*, functions as a cultural product, and it becomes ontologically maligned because play is merely derivative, *not* a necessary activity.[61]

Clearly this is not Plato's own account which assumes that play is an existentiale and not merely a derivative feature of the human condition. However, this materialist view (e.g., of Democritus) has interesting political implications, because it sidesteps the Platonic question of what constitutes good play and raises instead the problem of who can afford to engage in a leisurely playful lifestyle. In this context, play becomes ideologically suspect, as an activity that is only consummated by the economic-political elites.

In the *Laws*, while play is at the forefront of the conversation, the play perspective shifts slightly in favor of an Apollonian order. Similarly, the style of the conversation is markedly nonconfrontational; thus the Platonic dialogue "succeeds" in setting itself apart from an eristic interrogation. Play, again, is contrasted with seriousness, but an ethical polarization is absent. In jest *and* seriousness, the Stranger remarks that play is what makes a human life bearable and in fact it is the most divine aspect of humans (803b). A citation of the *paignon*-simile from Book I might serve to illustrate this point:

> May we not regard every living being as a puppet of the gods, which may be their plaything only, or may be created with a purpose; for that is a matter which we cannot certainly know? But this we know, that these affections in us are like cords and strings, which pull us different and opposite ways, and to opposite actions; and herein lies the difference between virtue and vice. (644d-e)

Plato then ponders what happens if this puppet is put into a state of drunkenness, which alternatively raises the interesting question whether these playthings are ever sobered up enough to engage with the "truth"—a question picked up by Hegel's trope of the Bacchanalian revel in *The Phenomenology of Spirit*.

In light of the abundance of play metaphors in the *Laws*, one might want to toy with the idea that Plato's harsh discrediting of playful mimesis only is a *comic* aberration. After all, the "theologia ludens" passage solemnly holds that "man is made God's plaything, and that is the best part in him." And "life must be lived as play, playing certain games, making sacrifices, etc." (803c-d). This passage hardly suggests that mimetic play has to be ruled out. No such ontological prescriptions are invoked here (although it is not specified which are the "certain," "most beautiful" games to be played). Note also that Plato does not use new terms—to make room for "authentic" play—unlike Aristotle, who discards *paidia* but praises *schole*, to elevate the true, pure play of philosophers and priests. Spariosu aptly calls Plato's dialogues "paignia"—the "trying out and testing" of his thought, in particular of his conception of play, which is reflected on further in the *Republic* and the *Laws*.[62]

In this chapter I attempted to contribute to a ludic reevaluation of Plato's work, by drawing on critical insights made by Nietzsche, Fink, Deleuze, and Derrida but also by offering a "misreading" or a "spoiling" of their anti-Platonic play. *Paidia*, for the most part, does not get maligned as mere play in order to be contrasted with serious activities; rather, several dialogues seem to attest to the conflation of these opposites; on the other hand, I want to note that Plato favors an ethical polarization of good and bad play, and an ontological benediction of play as an existentiale, "as being the best in man." Furthermore, Plato does not eclipse the Dionysian ludic element from his philosophy, and we see evidence for that claim in Socrates' play with masks, i.e., his toying with the sophists and his defense of philosophical madness in the *Phaedrus*. I argue that mimetic play is indeed important insofar as it shows Socrates' superb cunning when he imitates the sophists and beats his opponents at their own game. Play of representation (*Vorstellungsspiel*) becomes pretense-play (*Verstellungsspiel*). Both notions are captured in mimesis. In his (serious) pursuit of truth Plato gives a taste of his comic side by toying with masquerading and by seducing us with regulatory fictions. An account of truth may be represented in myth-telling but those myths might also mask the truth (e.g., the Myth of Theuth)—this is Plato's esoteric appeal which infuriated Aristotle. The Socratic satyric mask does hide "something" which can be uncovered and claimed, through various means, e.g., irony, buffoonery. In that sense, it is not yet a trickster, a coyote, who knows very well that there is no real self once a mask is peeled off. Only Hegel's "tarrying with the negative" will reveal that there is no essence behind the mask—philosophers have to come to terms with playing "merely" with masquerades, simulacra. And Nietzsche, the artist-metaphysician, fully grasps this affirmative, yet subversive, dimension of the thinking muse.

Clearly, there is no room for transgression in Socratic philosophy. He toys with poetic, sexualized images of madness (e.g., in *Ion* and *Charmides*) but always assumes a reflective pose so that philosophy does not get tainted by such impurity, does not really get out of control. Temperance always ought to be the guiding principle. Hence Apollonian play prevails—but still, lurking (as if from behind the mask), there is a possibility of toying with the Dionysian where Plato cannot operate as the absolute spin meister.

Notes

1. Cf. Eugen Fink, *Spiel als Weltsymbol* (Stuttgart, 1960) and Rainer Marten, who notes: "Play needs a being-for [*Voreinander*] and a being-with [*Miteinander*]" (personal communication). Cf. also Marten on the importance of love being a mise-en-scène, a performative, radically haphazard play (*Selbstinszenierung* and a *va banque* kind of play) (*Lebenskunst* [München: Wilhelm Fink Verlag, 1993], 178).

2. Cf. Susan Levin, "Woman's Nature and Role in the Ideal *Polis*: *Republic V* Revisited," in *Feminism and Ancient Philosophy*, ed. Julia Ward (New York: Routledge,

1996), 15-18.

3. Such is Derrida's view in his article "Plato's Pharmacy" (in *Dissemination*, trans. Barbara Johnson, [Chicago: University of Chicago, 1981], 156).

4. Cf. Elin Diamond's insightful discussion of the question: "can there be a feminist mimesis?" taking a cue from Irigaray's critique of Platonic specular operation in her "Mimesis, Mimicry, and the 'True-Real'" (in *Modern Drama* 32 (1989): 58-72). Cf. also Froma Zeitlin, "Playing the Other: Theater, Theatricality, and the Feminine in Greek Drama," *Representations* II (1985): 63-94.

5. In this regard I disagree with Derrida who claims that whenever play serves as (serious *pharmakon* (e.g., in the *Phaedrus*), it has already lost its playful appeal—in the name of logos or truth (Derrida, *Disseminations*, 156).

6. In the *Republic* Plato also discusses play qua *paideia* (education, pedagogy), thus highlighting play's instrumental function (cf. Book II). A discussion of this important feature of *paidia* is beyond the scope of this chapter. I will attend to it in the Aristotle chapter (Chapter 3).

7. Mimesis, according to Grube's translation, is used in the sense of "impersonation" in book III (G. M. Grube, *Plato's Republic* [Indianapolis: Hackett, 1974, 63, n.21).

8. Unless otherwise indicated, I will follow Grube's translation (1974).

9. Cf. Brecht on the alienation effect in *Brecht on Theatre* (New York: Hill & Wang), 37.

10. Deleuze, *Difference and Repetition*, 1994, 245. I am grateful to Andrew Cutrofello for pointing out this remark.

11. Fink, 1960, 89-117.

12. Fink, 1960, 101.

13. Fink, 1960, 110.

14. Fink, 1960, 89.

15. On this point, cf. Hermann Gundert's analysis: "Plato's polemic was directed primarily against that what is played [*Gespieltes*], which pretends to be serious, rather than against playing per se" ("Zum Spiel bei Platon," in *Beispiele. Festschrift für E. Fink*, 1965, my translation), 210.

16. Joachim Dalfen, *Polis und Poiesis: Die Auseinandersetzung mit der Dichtung bei Platon und seinen Zeitgenossen* (München: Wilhelm Fink Verlag, 1974), 266.

17. Cf. Dalfen, 1974, 315.

18. Undue hasty play-production also is rebuked in the simile of the garden of Adonis in *Phaedrus* 276b. It is contrasted with serious time-consuming labor. (See discussion below.)

19. Note that Plato was an accomplished comedy writer before he met Socrates. Since Plato holds comedy in higher esteem than tragedy or epos, Nietzsche blames Socrates/Plato for initiating the decline of tragic, Dionysian art form and elevating the Appolonian, rationalistic art form of comedy (cf. "Birth of Tragedy," in *Basic Writings*, trans., ed., W. Kaufmann, [New York: Random House, 1968], passim).

20. Cf. Grube (1974, 241, n.4) who suggests, *au contraire*, not to take Plato's illustration about the gods too seriously.

21. On the positive uses of perplexity in philosophical thinking, cf. Matthews, "Vom Nutzen der Perplexität: Denken lehren mithilfe der Philosophie" in *Rostock Philosophische Schriften* (1996).

22. Cf. William Desmond, *Beyond Hegel and Dialectic* (New York: SUNY, 1992), 256. However, Desmond also claims that Plato's Socrates is the first philosopher to laugh at himself, 260. Desmond seems to misunderstand the purpose of Socrates' masks (e.g.,

of self-deprecation). I think that one of its functions is to obfuscate his elenctic method by disarming, duping the opponent, who realizes too late that his arguments are refuted (by the sophist himself!).

23. Wendy Brown, "'Supposing Truth Were a Woman . . .': Plato's Subversion of Masculine Discourse," in *Feminist Interpretations of Plato*, ed. Nancy Tuana (University Park, Pa.: Penn State, 1994), 159.

24. I owe this point to John Brentlinger.

25. This is also Brown's position, 159.

26. Cf. Luce Irigaray, "Sorcerer Love: A Reading of Plato's *Symposium*, Diotima's Speech," in *Feminist Interpretations of Plato*, ed. Nancy Tuana, trans. Eleanor H. Kuykendall, (University Park, Pa.: Penn State, 1994) and Andrea Nye, "Irigaray and Diotima at Plato's Symposium" (in *Feminist Interpretations of Plato*, ed. Nancy Tuana (University Park, Pa.: Penn State, 1994).

27. To my knowledge one does not know whether or not this is a historic figure.

28. Cf. John Brentlinger, who expounds on a point made by Helen Bacon ("Socrates Crowned," in *The Virginia Quarterly Review*, V [1959]: 415-30) that Plato casts Agathon and Socrates as opponents. Their speeches on love are made in honor of Dionysus who presides as judge over this *agon* (contest) in John Brentlinger, *The Symposium of Plato*, trans. Suzy Q.Groden (Amherst: University of Massachusetts, 1970), 4.

29. Brentlinger, 1970, 4.

30. On an analysis of satyric imagery on Greek vases, cf. Francois Lissarrague "The Sexual Life of Satyrs" in *Before Sexuality: The Construction of Erotic Experience in the Ancient Greek World*, ed. D. Halperin et al. (Princeton: Princeton University, 1990).

31. Elias, *Plato's Defense of Poetry* (Albany: SUNY, 1984), 37. However, one could argue with Elias, that he should perhaps be listening more sceptically to the ironic tone of Socrates' assertion that rhetoric has 'greater power' over uncertain things, such as myths, than the dialectic (*Phaedr.* 263b).

32. Deleuze, *Difference and Repetition*, 1994, 61.

33. While I will not discuss the question why Socrates uses myths in the *Phaedrus*, the following passage presents a compelling interpretation: "A myth, unlike a syllogism, has the capacity to act as a complex mirror in which people can recognize not just who they are but who they might become at their best. Platonic myth is a mirror that can not only reflect one's hopes but also seek to realize them. While it preserves contact with our ordinary self-understanding, it also deepens it" (Charles Griswold, *Self-Knowledge in Plato's Phaedrus* [New Haven, Conn.: Yale University, 1986], 147).

34. Derrida, 1981, 68.

35. Myth may however fit neatly into logocentrism, according to Deleuze: "For if it is true that, within Platonism in general, myth and dialectic are distinct forces, this distinction no longer matters once dialectic discovers its true method in division. Division overcomes this duality and integrates myth into the dialectic; it makes myth an element of the dialectic itself" (Deleuze, *Difference and Repetition*, 61).

36. On this point of originality, cf. Frutinger, *Les Mythes de Platon* (Paris: Alcan, 1930), quoted in Derrida (1981), 67.

37. On this point, cf. Griswold, 1986, 139-40.

38. Note here the parallel to Hesiod's story of Pandora, the gift/poison from the gods to the humans.

39. Derrida suggests that Socrates plays the role of a *pharmakeus* (magician), cf. *Symposium* (being confronted with a "J'accuse" by Agathon and Alcibiades of bewitching them), *Meno* (allegory of Socrates being a sting ray numbing body and soul

of Meno), *Charmides* (handing out the charm that relieves Charmides of his headaches), 117-19.

40. Derrida, 1981, 93.

41. On the meaning of the gardens of Adonis see the translators' comments in Plato, *Phaedrus*, trans. Nehemas and Woodruff (Indianapolis: Hackett, 1995), 81, n.184.

42. Compare this allegory with the deed of the painter, mentioned in Book X of the *Republic* who hurries around and *quickly* copies down images with his mirror.

43. Cf. Derrida, 1981, 154-55.

44. Brown, 1994, 163.

45. Brown, 1994, 170.

46. Similarly, whenever Slavoj Zizek wants to convey a "serious" point, he reverts to jokes in his writings on Hegel, psychoanalysis and Hitchcock.

47. Paul Friedländer, *Platon: Seinswahrheit und Lebenswirklichkeit* (Berlin: de Gruyter, 1954), 152.

48. Friedländer, 1954, 154.

49. However, in the aporetic dialogues, Socrates avers, with sincerity, that he is also perplexed, e.g., about what virtue is (cf. *Meno*). On this point, see Gareth Matthews, "The Uses of Perplexity: Teaching Thinking Through Philosophy" (ms.).

50. On this point, cf. Sprague's explanation, 1993, 61, n.104.

51. I am grateful to Gareth Matthews for a discussion of the Platonic examples mentioned below.

52. Jowett's translation.

53. Cf. María Lugones's seminal paper "Playfulness, 'World'-travelling, and Loving Perception," *Hypatia*, 2, no. 2 (1987): 3-19.

54. Cf. Dalfen, 1974, 300-307.

55. Oddly, Spariosu does not reflect on the gendered nature of the dichotomies he invokes, although I hesitate to label the Presocratic period as dominating with "male" values and the Socratic epoch being imbued with the "feminine" play spirit. Such talk of polarization is clearly essentialist and disguises its intent to set up a "better," more authentic ontological mode of play.

56. Ryle, *Plato's Progress* (Cambridge: Cambridge University, 1966), 10.

57. GMN, 1991, 178.

58. GMN, 1991, 189.

59. Cf. my discussion above (chapter 1).

60. In the *Republic*, pretend-play has a different valence: Dialectics out to be taught to adolescents *as if* it were a game (536e-37a).

61. Cf. Gundert, "Zum Spiel bei Platon," 73.

62. GMN, 1991, 168.

Chapter 3

ARISTOTLE'S MALEDICTION OF PLAY

Plato presents us with a complex picture of *paidia*. He clearly shows the need to authenticate activities of the philosopher over and against those of the sophists; the prize always goes towards the true (and always sober) player.[1] Yet, playfulness is an intrinsic value which is "the best part in humans"—spoilsports do not have to be sorted out. Plato's strenuous effort to instigate devaluation, if not malediction, of play loses its semiotic force slipping on the Dionysian surface (or is it an abyss?) while searching for the right kind of play. Regardless of the author's intention, it is simply misguided to suggest that Plato ultimately maligns play. Nietzsche's and Fink's critiques fail to acknowledge the performative aspects of irony, of myths and masks, and the presence of Dionysian impulses in the Platonic dialogue.

It is Aristotle who relegates the Dionysian aspects in Plato's play to "abstract negation" and strengthens the Apollonian motif in play—what Spariosu calls the logo-rational principle. So, it is Aristotle, not Plato, who instigates a malediction of play. This seems to be a peculiar claim; after all, Aristotle validates (poetic) mimesis which Plato dismisses from his polis. Since mimesis is a kind of play, how is it possible to maintain that Aristotle denounces playfulness? To underscore this claim we will look at how Aristotle sets up his (philosophical) game vis-à-vis play, leisure, and mimesis in his ethical, political, and aesthetic writings. In particular, we need to consider whether *paidia* is validated and affirmed instrumentally, or rather autotelically, i.e., pursued for its own sake.

Maligning Play in the *Nicomachean Ethics*

In the *Nicomachean Ethics* (EN) we see a surprising attack on *paidia*. Playfulness is maligned in a way that sets Aristotle markedly apart from his teacher's account of play. The EN discusses the various ways a virtuous person can attain happiness (*eudaimonia*).[2] Aristotle guides us from a discussion of different kinds of virtue (pertaining to the practical-ethical life) to the best kind (realized in the theoretical life of the philosopher); the latter is presented in Book X (6-9) of the EN, in which Aristotle outlines his conception of the highest happiness. It is only within this context of mapping out the best life, *bios theoretikos*, that Aristotle introduces the concepts of play and leisure. In order to understand *paidia* with respect to the rational ideal life mapped out in the EN, it is paramount to focus on these passages—especially chapters 6 and 7—in the last book of the EN.[3]

In chapter 6 of Book X, Aristotle questions the nature of happiness (1176a30; cf. EN I.6). Happiness is thought to be self-sufficient, Aristotle observes, and desirable for its own sake; yet, virtuous actions also belong to happiness. The activity[4] of happiness has to be contrasted, Aristotle goes on, with playful ones, contrary to the dominant opinion. To put it simply, striving for happiness does not consist of indulging in amusement (1176b9). This instruction is in stark contrast to the Homeric and Heraclitean predilection for the aristocratic life, clearly synonomous with indulging in play—not toil. But here in the EN, Aristotle admonishes his audience (the corrupt archons, *phauloi*, supporting the tyrant ruler) that a life in accordance with virtue is serious and not childish play: "And we say that serious things [*spoudaia*] are better than laughable things and those connected with amusement [*paidia*] . . ." (1177a). Aristotle affirms here unambiguously that play and seriousness are opposites. *Paidia* signifies trivial pursuit, cheap amusement in these passages of the EN;[5] in fact, "to exert oneself and work for the sake of amusement [*paidia*] seems silly and utterly childish" (1176b). Moreover, playing games for amusement's sake is contrasted with "serious" activities of the virtuous person (in chapter 6), the philosopher (in chapter 7), and the legislator (in chapter 9); play is also cast in opposition to work (*ergon*). Altogether, Aristotle maligns play seven times in chapter 6, and it is only twice, in connection with the notion of proper relaxation, that he notes its beneficial consequences.

It is difficult to conceptualize play as having any intrinsic value; the situations that are described which allow for the introjection of play merely point to its instrumental validation. Thus, a child's play may be valued because it is pedagogically useful,[6] and adults may also engage in play for the sake of relaxation "because we cannot work continuously" (1176b).[7] Play thus is valued for other purposes—it is not an activity worth seeking for itself.

What then is it that philosophers do, if not to play discursively, to toy with opponents, as so brilliantly done by Socrates? Aristotle reserves better things to the rational pursuit in life. Philosophers don't play, not even monologically. They *contemplate*—albeit leisurely. As Desmond (1992) notes, leisure is highly valued and sets the philosopher's activities apart from others. Thus it reaffirms the hierarchical nature of the different ways of life that Aristotle delineates in his discussion of happiness. Leisure is cast as an opposite of work and characterized by the absence of external, material constraints. In comparing Hegel to Aristotle, Desmond suggests:

> Without denying work's necessity, the speculative Hegel, with Aristotle, looks to the end of toil in the highest activity, an activity not itself instrumental work but leisure. Philosophy looks to leisure, is itself leisure, *skole*, an activity enjoyed as an end in itself, a goal whole within itself, yet open, making the human being at

home with being's otherness. As Aristotle piously puts it: A man living in philosophical leisure lives not as a mere man but as having the divine dwelling with
him.[8]

Schole has a special status as an activity of the philosopher, who after all engages in theoretical, scientific matters and whose life characterizes the best life.
Amélie O. Rorty concedes that if it is the case that theoretical and practical rea-
soning clash, theoretical deliberation takes precedence, "because the independence of the intellectual from the moral virtues allows contemplation to continue
in the midst of political disaster and practical blindness."[9] As a second best life,
Aristotle proposes the political life of the lawmaker. The legislator after all uses
phronesis (practical reason),[10] so that his intellectual requirements are similar to
that of the philosopher; therefore, the *nomothetes* also requires leisure.

It is only in the life of the many, who engage in "many games," when *paidia*
(playful amusements) takes precedence over *schole*. My delineation of the three
lives in Book X of the EN differs from the one proposed by Sparshott (1994),
insofar as he seems to suggest that playful diversions of the *phauloi* can be characterized as leisure activities: The life of pleasure is leisurely but not serious, the
life of moral virtue is serious but not leisurely, the life of the intellect has both
values (and from this point of view represents perhaps the most complete
[*teleios*] virtue as well as the most exalted).[11] I think that Sparshott is correct in
pointing out that *spoude* does not need to be an opposite of *schole* in Aristotle.
The processes of ontological malediction of play (*paidia*)—and the concurrent
benediction of seriousness (*spoude*)—are revealed in the coupling of the following concepts: play and frivolity, relaxation and seriousness, and finally, leisure and seriousness.

First, *paidia* qua childishness, amusement, and pastime cannot be taken seriously. The play of children and the hedonistic doings of the inferior adults
(*phauloi*) are "frivolous matters." To engage in play for its own sake becomes a
suspicious act and is assigned the lowest rank in the hierarchy of ethical activities. Second, the virtuous, hardworking serious person combines *spoude* and
diagoge (relaxation); still, the virtuous activities of the *spoudaios* are classified
merely as secondary in the ontological order, because this "practical life" is re-
active and too caught up with urgent political and economic matters. Thus the
life of such a person is not self-sufficient enough to be considered the best life.
Third, the philosopher's contemplative activities are considered to be of the
highest rank because they combine *spoude* and *schole* vis-à-vis the demands of a
theoretical life (*bios theoretikos*) which is sufficiently independent from external
constraints. In this context *schole* has no connotations of Dionysian frenzy or
playfulness. It is noteworthy that the hierarchy of playfulness corresponds to the
three lives outlined in Book I and X: the pleasurable life of the *phauloi*, the life
of the virtuous person who deals with serious matters (*spoudaia*), and finally,
the life of the philosopher, which eclipses the need for play qua amusement altogether.

However, some scholars have argued that Aristotle conflates playfulness
with leisure activity, an interpretation which would contribute to a more ambivalent reading of his harsh stance on play. Sparshott's book *Taking Life Seri-*

ously: A Study of the Argument of the Nicomachean Ethics (1994) is a case in point. He compares the following sayings, "We are busy that we may have leisure" (*ascholoumetha hina scholazomen*, 1177b5) and Anarcharsis's advice "to play in order to be serious" (*paizein hopos spoudazei*, 1176b33).[12] Aristotle, no doubt, is comfortable with juxtaposing these proverbs, which to Sparshott seem contradictory. Sparshott claims that the tension is only resolved in the discussion of pleasure in the *Rhetoric*. He points to I.11, a discussion of the nature of pleasure. Aristotle states there that strain and serious effort are eliminated from the consideration (of pleasant matters), since, unless one is accustomed to them, they are painful and have to do with compulsion and force. Moreover, the opposites of work and seriousness are those activities associated with play: "ease, freedom from toil, relaxation, amusement, rest, and sleep" (*Rhet.* 1370a). Sparshott, however, does not comment on the fact that leisure is not included in this list. In illustrating the pleasure associated with playing agonistic games, Aristotle remarks that the learning of "serious games" (as opposed to ball, dice, and draught games) might not be always pleasant from the start, but once they are a habit they become pleasant. As an example of such a serious game he mentions hunting with hounds (*Rhet.* 1371a3-5). By differentiating between serious and nonserious games, Aristotle seems to indicate that the involvement in some games may throw the contestant into grave danger.

Contrasting, as he does, these "play" passages in the EN and the *Rhetoric*, Sparshott does not notice that, in the list of playful diversions in the *Rhetoric*, leisure is notably absent because Aristotle does not consider it being part of *paidia*. In fact, Aristotle quite clearly differentiates the notion of play (*paidia*, *diagoge*) from leisure (*schole*). Hence, what presented itself as an irresolvable tension is actually nothing of the sort. On the other hand, leisure and seriousness are contiguous, not oppositional concepts, as Aristotle's descriptions of the life of contemplation attest to. The qualities describing a life of *theoria*, that is, a life of highest happiness, which are contiguous with leisure as well, are stability, pleasure, seriousness, independence, and final telos (cf. EN 1177a18-b26); his play (or is it work?) is a scientific activity, a serious pursuit of the conditions of knowledge. The theoretical life is thus marked by leisurely activity sought for its own sake.

In order to set up this worthy game of attaining happiness, Aristotle has to start out with a malediction of play, insofar as it is merely pleasurable and childish, (*paidion hai hedeiai*) and clearly not an activity of theoretical reflection. *Schole* has more to do with strenuous academic work than with "mere" play and is carefully delineated as being accessible only to the few, i.e., to those who bother to inquire about metaphysical and ethical questions. *Schole* is a necessary condition for the person who wants to engage with a book such as the EN! Sparshott points out correctly that Aristotle basically describes the material conditions of philosophers, or of priests, who are—due to the division of labor— the designated leisure class.[13] Eschewing the (ethical and political) question of their parasitic status, Aristotle simply affirms leisure as worthy contemplating activity. Desmond's emphatic pronouncement notwithstanding (see his quote above), it is clearly not the case that the meaning of *schole* encompasses the

Hegelian notion of the Bacchanalian revel,[14] since Aristotle's *schole* illustrates Apollonian order and harmony (*kosmos*) and clearly banishes Dionysian aspects. The *Nicomachean Ethics* initiates a malediction of play, of Dionysian play—a theme continued in the *Politics* and *Poetics*.

Two Kinds of Play in the *Politics*

In the *Politics*[15] Aristotle explores the moral and political conduct of an individual virtuous person vis-à-vis a virtuous self-fulfillment in the community (*oikos*). In the context of prescribing norms for a political community, the valence of *paidia* ought to shift as well. After all, the ethical horizon of (quasi-solitary) philosophical musings is quite distinct from the civic responsibilities of a *nomothetes* (legislator) who might perceive certain (pedagogical) needs being fulfilled in child's play.

In Book VII and VIII, Aristotle continues his discussion of children's play and of philosophical leisurely activities. Again, as postulated in the EN, leisure is contrasted with *paidia* (play, pastime). However, what is different is that "diversion," as Spariosu points out correctly, in Aristotle's play theory differs from Plato insofar as the Stagirite no longer views intellectual diversion (*diagoge*) as a form of *paidia*. In its highest expression *diagoge* amounts to philosophizing.[16] This semiotic hierarchy is analogous to the benediction of leisure at the expense of *paidia* in the EN, that is, in Aristotle's reevaluation of leisure as a specific attribute of the philosophical life.

The hierarchies of "playful" activities are especially pronounced in Book VIII, in which *scholia* (leisure) is ranked highest, followed by *ascholia* (work—for sake of leisure), *anapausis* (recreation), and lastly, *paidia* (play, amusement).[17] Aristotle's differentiated validation of these kinds of activities is consistent with his argumentation on play and leisure in the EN. In the *Politics* as in the EN, a leisurely activity is associated most of all with the "work" of the philosopher, which is distinct from the demands of practical life: "For many necessaries of life have to be supplied before we can have leisure . . . as the proverb says, 'There is no leisure for slaves,' and those who cannot face danger like men are the slaves of any invader. Courage and endurance are required for business and philosophy for leisure . . ." (VII, 1334a18-24). Philosophical life is not preoccupied with material conditions but is compared to a life of blissfulness. However, Aristotle emphasizes a different point here: in the absence of war and external impediments, it is essential to get exposed to philosophy (and temperance and justice), so as not to live superfluously. In this case, philosophy seems to fill a void (which of course for the ancient poets was filled with playing games . . .) (1334a30-34).

Similarly, Aristotle falls back conveniently on his dichotomy of *bios theoretikos* and *bios praktikos* by advocating a division between the upper and lower agora in the city: the life of the upper agora is devoted to leisure and free from the tumultous thriving of *hoi polloi*, whereas the lower marketplace, the traders' area, is devoted to the necessities of life (VII, 1331b). Life thus is divided into business and leisure, where only *schole* is an end in itself. In the same vein, Ar-

istotle determines that there are two kinds of spectators and, thus, various per-
formances are needed to satisfy both of them: There are free and educated spectators (supposedly priests and philosophers) and the vulgar crowd (of artisans).
The latter should be entertained by professional musicians, who practice art
merely in order to give pleasure, not to give educational enjoyment (1342a).
Who performs for the former crowd of nobles? Aristotle does not tell us—but
most likely they "play" for their own kind: fellow philosophers who are free
from the constraints of taking care of material necessities so that they do not
need to perform in order to earn an income.[18]

In the end of Book VII and in Book VIII, the pedagogy of playfulness is
reconsidered. Yet, this reconsideration occurs within the parameters of Aristotle's prescriptions with respect to *proper* children's education (*paideia*). He
notes that their play "should not be vulgar, tiring or effeminate" (VII, 1336a27-
28).[19] In a lengthy discussion of the merits of music for children's education,
Aristotle decides in its favor, because of its "power of forming the character"
(1340b11-12). However, Aristotle worries about the varied uses of music; it can
lend itself to either Dionysian (=bad) pleasure or to Apollonian (=good, intellectual) pleasure. Music may produce education (*paideia*), amusement (*paidia*),
or intellectual enjoyment (*diagoge*): "Amusement is for the sake of relaxation,
and relaxation is of necessity sweet, for it is the remedy of pain caused by toil;
and intellectual enjoyment is universally acknowledged to contain an element
not only of the noble but of the pleasant, for happiness is made up of both"
(1339b15-19).

Clearly, all three concepts are theorized as pertaining to Apollonian values
only. In the case of *paidia*, this means that it is properly made rational: play has
instrumental value; that is, we play in order to perform better at work. Spariosu
maintains that Aristotle gives a circular argument, because work and play do not
exist only for the sake of leisure, but also for the sake of each other.[20] Unlike in
the EN, Aristotle links amusement or pastimes with "proper" recreation (*anapausis*) in this passage. *Diagoge*, synonymous with happiness, consists of play
and relaxation and in this context becomes "intellectualized." However,
Spariosu's claim of circularity is puzzling. Work, Aristotle states, does not exist
for the sake of amusement, and playing is merely an "alleviation of past toils
and pains" (*Pol.* 1339b39)—an admonishment which echoes the paidiophobic
passages of the EN.[21] However, people like to deviate from the path prescribed
by the philosopher. Aristotle notes: "It sometimes happens that men make
amusement the end, for the end probably contains some element of pleasure,
though not any ordinary or lower pleasure; but they mistake the lower for the
higher, and in seeking for the one find the other, since every pleasure has a like-
ness to the end of action"(*Pol.* 1339b32-35). Even though such playful amusement is not an end in itself, engaging in it is a harmless, excusable activity. After
all, the act of listening to music is relaxing and intellectually stimulating.

When properly sanctioned, music education ought to pay attention to building moral character and the music to be played ought to avoid stimulating base
desires ("Bacchic frenzy"!) which are produced by flute playing (*Pol.*, VIII,
1341a).[22] The main impetus for the lengthy discussion of the purposefulness of

music education/play seems to be to drive out the Dionysian element, which is best achieved by means of catharsis or purgation (cf. *Pol.* 1341b37; also *Poetics*, 1449b27). Those feeble minds who succumb to religious frenzy experience cathartic relief through listening to sacred songs. Members of the lower class whose "minds are perverted from the natural state" need to receive melodies in "perverted modes and highly strung and unnaturally coloured" (*Pol.* 1342a23-25). While Aristotle stresses the importance of play in music education, play is subservient to other activities, e.g., education does not occur for the sake of play, so that play has merely an instrumental value. It seems that if Aristotle could have conceived a way to get children to learn without pretend-play,[23] he would have preferred that!

Aristotle seems eager to set up a dichotomy between the play of children and "ordinary" people on the one hand and the edifying leisurely "play" of the philosopher and statesman on the other. He presents a multitude of examples for rationalizing and reifying this dichotomy, e.g., by claiming that the many simply enjoy perverted pleasures and are unable to become productive citizens. In outlining the best form of government, Aristotle maintains that "the citizens must not lead the life of mechanics or tradesmen, for such a life is ignoble, and inimical to virtue. Neither must they be husbandmen,[24] since leisure is necessary both for the development of virtue and the performance of political duties" (*Pol.* VII, 1328b39-1329a2). For Aristotle, the content of each play (of the two classes) is radically different from each other, and the play of the leisure class is clearly to be favored[25]; however, unlike in the EN, the other kind of play is also condoned in the *Politics*.

The play set up by Aristotle in his ethical and political writings has significant sociopolitical implications, insofar as it determines whose play is worthy of philosophical approval. This need for authenticating play has left its traces in Western discourse. A critical reevaluation of the Aristotelian validation of certain kinds of play occurs only in Marxist, phenomenological, deconstructivist play theories and in the novel field of the philosophy of childhood.[26]

Play and Mimesis in the *Poetics*

In order to address the question of whether Aristotle's *Poetics*[27] furthers a malediction of play, I will explore his analysis of how mimesis functions in poetic works.

Mimesis, Aristotle notes, is an intrinsic value, a characteristic of human nature: "Imitation is natural to man from childhood," and humans are the "most imitative creature[s] in the world, and learn . . . first by imitation. And it is also natural for all to delight in works of imitation" (1448b). Imitation is inherently playful. (Note that Aristotle adopts Plato's definition of mimesis as "a kind of play.") The poets portray human actions in three different ways, i.e., they either idealize them, make caricatures of them, or portray them realistically. The most common imitative poetic works are epic poetry and tragedy, both representing noble actions, and comedy, representing ridiculous actions (1447a-1448a). After discussing the differences between these imitative arts, Aristotle focuses on tragic art (chapters 6-22) and ends with a brief discussion of epic art, claiming that tragedy is a superior kind of imitation to epic poetry (chapters 23-26) because it is better able to attain "the poetic effect than the Epic" (cf. 1462b). In assessing the value of poetry Aristotle makes use of ontological categories, such as plausibility, possibility, and reality, to elevate the status of poetry, which portrays the plausible and general, as being a more philosophic and serious techne than history. Possibility is ontologically approved, whereas actuality, pertaining to mere singular events, is maligned (9.1451b). However, it remains unclear if Aristotle includes comedy here, as a "serious," i.e., grave, techne. Given the importance of poetry in comparison to historic accounts of events, it would seem that Aristotle also elevates mimesis (and play). But what kind of mimesis is restored in tragic art?

Spariosu correctly holds that it is misleading to suggest—as Anglo-American scholarship has done—that Aristotle restores the prestige of mimesis in the context of poetry.[28] He states that in fact Aristotle continues to emphasize median values over archaic ones and that both Aristotle and Plato see poetry as a playful simulation (mimesis) of serious discourse and that poetry produces pleasure, not knowledge. However, I think that we need to differentiate between Aristotle's and Plato's uses of mimesis insofar as for Aristotle a poem's purpose is not knowledge but only plausibility whereas for Plato true mimesis is indeed "philosophical" and produces intellectual enjoyment. I also argue against Spariosu (1991) who holds that Aristotle continues the Platonic taming of the ecstatic nature of poetic play.[29] In fact, unlike Aristotle, Plato does not condemn poetic frenzy or divine rapture, but he sees its truest expression in the philosophical enthusiast, who is also engaged in poetic mimesis. Furthermore, Plato does not chastise divine madness in poets but demands that philosophers examine the poems critically.[30]

In contrast to Plato, Aristotle favors the intelligent, talented (*euphues*) poet who puts himself into the roles he creates over the mad, frenzied poet, since the latter fails to stay within the boundaries of human experience, and just creates whatever he imagines, i.e., without any purposefulness. Aristotle writes:

> At the time when he is constructing his Plots . . . the poet should remember . . . to put the actual scenes as far as possible before his eyes. In this way, seeing everything with the vividness of an eye-witness as it were, he will devise what is appropriate, and be least likely to overlook incongruities. (17.1455a)

Aristotle envisions a poet, who shrewdly maps out the details of his plot in his imagination and makes them as plausible as possible. Aristotle also acknowledges that a good poet, who is passionately attached to his plot and characters, may portray their emotions more convincingly:

> As far as may be, too, the poet should even act his story with the very gestures of his personages. Given the same natural qualifications, he who feels the emotions to be described will be the most convincing; distress and anger, for instance, are portrayed most truthfully by one who is feeling them at the moment.

> Hence it is that poetry demands a man with a special gift for it, or else one with a touch of madness in him; the former can easily assume the required mood, and the latter may be actually beside himself with emotion [=*ekstatikoi*]. (17.1455a)

To create a poetic work with sentiments of madness is acceptible to Aristotle if it is effective in purging the spectator's emotions. However, given the restrictions Aristotle places on the poet's mimetic production, it is clear that Bacchic frenzy is to be tamed, as Spariosu suggests. For instance, a poet's portrayal of the very bad villain attaining a bad state is not condoned, because it does not produce the proper emotions, namely fear or pity, in the spectator (1453a).[31]

The theatre critic Augusto Boal (1979) goes a step further in his critique of Aristotle's instrumental-rational treatment of poetry. In the chapter "Aristotle's Coercive System of Tragedy" (in *Theatre of the Oppressed*), he argues that Aristotle justifies the use of tragedy as an instrument of repression to avoid instability among the populace which might be discontent about existing socioeconomic injustice. The stabilizing function of tragedy consists in the sympathetic portrayal of the tragic hero as being smitten with a tragic flaw (*hamartia*) and after his recognition of his error suffering the consequences (*catastrophe*). Most importantly, the spectator, who is terrified by the catastrophe, needs to experience *catharsis*, i.e., he has to be purified from his own *hamartia*.[32] Spectators live vicariously the hero's experiences.[33] They empathize with him and at the same time fear that they too suffer from an impure character, from bad traits. In instilling this fear of excessive, unlawful acts tragedy effectively normalizes behavior and produces docile bodies.

Instead of providing us with a conception of poetic play, in which creativity, spontaneity, and a giddy play with seriousness surface,[34] Aristotle prescribes a (best) play that ought to engender proper feelings of terror and pity. Nevertheless he disavows that tragic, mimetic production has political significance. Aristotle, as Boal correctly notes, gives an ideological manifesto in defense of the status quo (of an undemocratic social system). Rather than romanticizing the "playful spirit" of Greek society (cf. Nietzsche, Huizinga), Boal has pointed out the socializing, repressive character of poetic performance, whose sole purpose is to enforce a rationalistic (Apollonian) aesthetic code, a standard which is employed for the "moral education of aesthetic man."[35] Mimetic representation of tragic aspects of human nature, human reality, is thus condemned to the "service of Reason."[36] A similar intellectual *Anspruch* is levied against the spectator. As McCumber points out, one has to be properly educated in order to experience tragic catharsis:

> Tragic catharsis is clearly connected to the pursuit of the Noble, because one who undergoes catharsis is always freeborn and educated. *Politics* 8.7 excludes from catharsis even those free men who follow trades, such as mechanics and laborers; denizens of the realm of necessity rather than of Nobility, they seek only relaxation from art [*Poetics* 1342a18ff.]. (McCumber 1988, 60)

A fortiori, women and slaves would also be unfit to experience catharsis—the latter because they follow trades; the former because they have no education.[37]

While Aristotle condones the idea that a poetic work should take seriously the realm of possibilities of human experience by exaggerating or accentuating certain tragic flaws, the main impetus of a superior mimetic performance is to present us with a rather limited trajectory of human emotions: a good tragic work has to incite pity or terror, and it may not deviate from this mandate. In addition it has to "induce" purgation (*catharsis*) of those feelings in the spectator in order to avoid promoting agonism and social unrest in the audience. It thus becomes clear that play is maligned when it deviates from the rationalist Apollonian path.

Clearly, in all of his writings, Aristotle eschews Dionysian and agonistic elements of play. While similar (moral) misgivings about the ludic god are voiced in the works of Hesiod, Aristophanes, and Plato, I maintain that it is Aristotle who consistently disavows the relevance of frenzy, cunning, and humor for leading a virtuous life. His Dionysian disavowal is most apparent in the persistent functional employment of *paidia*. Play is good only for relaxation in order to improve one's subsequent work habits. In the *Nicomachean Ethics*, the use of play varies for the many and for the virtuous person; by setting normative guidelines for the proper use of play, Aristotle introduces an unprecedented malediction of *paidia*: play becomes the Other of reason, due to the distinction drawn between *schole* and *paidia*. Aristotle effectively erases tragic play which—as Nietzsche points out—is both destructive and life-affirming (in "Birth of Tragedy," passim).

In the *Politics paidia* is represented above all as having instrumental value, especially in the context of the discussion of music education, yet, despite its seemingly higher ranking, play is an activity which ought not to be pursued for its own sake. Finally, in the *Poetics*, play qua "mimesis" seems to have intrinsic value.

Three different kinds of hierarchical ranking of play can be identified: first, in the *Nicomachean Ethics*, play is ranked lowest and is squarely denounced as an activity unworthy of a virtuous person; secondly, in the *Politics*, play is considered a "harmless" activity, which can be taken up for educational and recreational purposes by the youth and lower classes (the demos); and finally, in the *Poetics*, play gains a higher status. Aristotle sets up Apollonian, normative standards for play: the play for amusement, enjoyed by the masses, is valuable if it is not tainted by "bad" elements, i.e., Dionysian impulses. Thus in tragedy we find a play that is valued for its own sake, but it is appropriately purified.[38]

Aristotle ushers in rationalistic values, and sets up a game that is about making rational choices and following given rules. Even in the *Poetics*, mimetic play is neither about playing with the masks of Silenus nor about cunning and frivolity. Given this evaluation of playful attitudes and activities, I suggest that Aristotle eclipses the Dionysian element—(free) play becomes the Other of reason.[39] Only in Hegel do we see a reevaluation of the Dionysian (in the Bacchanalian revel), where play recognizes itself in Reason—as truth.

Notes

1. On this point, cf. Deleuze, *Difference and Repetition*, 1994.

2. Even feminist scholarship has avoided a systematic discussion of these issues. Cf. Marcia Homiak, "Feminism and Aristotle's Rational Ideal," in *Feminism and Ancient Philosophy*, ed. Julia Ward (New York: Routledge, 1996), 118-37.

3. I find it surprising that Spariosu, who has written extensively on play theory in the ancient Greek world, does not deal with Aristotle's ethics at all in his book *God of Many Names* (GMN, 1991). His Aristotle chapter is entitled: "Aristotle: Poetics, Politics, and Play."

4. Note that for Aristotle happiness is not a state of being, a particular disposition (*hexis*) but is an activity (*energeia*). It is not just about being free from external constraints that determines happiness.

5. Dirlmeier translates *paidia* as "Verspieltheit," which is perhaps more to the point. (Aristoteles, *Nikomachische Ethik*, trans. F. Dirlmeier [Stuttgart, Germany: Reclam, 1980].) It conveys a sense of being obsessed with playing, indulging in a game as children do who skip school and shy away from "real life" responsibilities; it is clearly laden with negative value judgments in a way that "amusement" is not.

6. Curiously, the benefits of child's play are not explicitly mentioned in his ethics. But we can infer this from the passages on education in the *Politics* (Book VII).

7. Incidentally, this sentiment is echoed in Kant (see Chapter 4 below).

8. Desmond, *Beyond Hegel and Dialectic* (New York: SUNY, 1992), 131.

9. Amélie Rorty, "The Place of Contemplation in Aristotle's *Nichomachian Ethics*," in *Essays on Aristotle's Ethics*, ed. Amélie Rorty (Los Angeles: UCLA, 1980), 392.

10. *Phronesis* is a virtue that has intrinsic status.

11. Francis Sparshott, *Taking Life Seriously: A Study of the Argument of the Nicomachean Ethics* (Toronto: University of Toronto, 1994), 332-33.

12. Sparshott, 1994, 430.

13. Sparshott 1994, 332.

14. On the notion of the revel, cf. my chapter on Hegel (Chapter 5).

15. I will follow Benjamin Jowett's translation for the most part.

16. GMN, 1991, 224.

17. Cf. GMN, 1991, 225-30.

18. Thus playing for money taints the value of this activity, a sentiment which reappears—emphatically!—in Huizinga, *Homo Ludens*.

19. This sexist admonishment echoes the *Republic*'s harsh indictment of the Homeric poets who are accused of stimulating effeminate sentiments with their wailings in the male audience.

20. GMN, 1991, 228.

21. In the EN, Aristotle attributes the misguided belief of valuing play as an end (rather than as a means) to the faulty deliberations and actions of the self-indulgent person, "the lover of amusement," who fails to realize that "amusement is a relaxation, since it is rest from work; and the lover of amusement is one of the people who go to excess in this" (EN, VII, 1150b16-18). Their excessive vice, Aristotle laments, is incurable (EN, 1150b32).

22. Most of this pedagogical discussion and the prescriptions of proper education Aristotle borrows from Plato's *Republic* and *Laws*.

23. I.e. a child's moral educator devises a "noble lie"—a play that isn't—in order to motivate the child to learn his chores.

24. To be condemned to the life of a househusband is unworthy of a free man. Since the *oikos* is the realm of the woman, he becomes "feminized." On this point, see McCumber's discussion of Oedipus's refusal to return to the palace, which is the "home, the crypt of woman." For it is better "to be an exile on the roads than a woman in the home" (John McCumber, "Aristotelian Catharsis and the Purgation of Woman," *Diacritics* Winter [1988]: 67).

25. Gareth Matthews' studies have shed a new light on this matter. He calls on adults to take children's philosophizing "seriously;" cf. *The Philosophy of Childhood* (1994); *Philosophy of the Young Child* (1980); and *Dialogues with Children* (1984).

26. I am thinking in particular of Buytendijk's work.

27. I will make use of Ingram Bywater's translation in R. McKeon, ed., *Basic Works of Aristotle* (New York: Random House, 1941).

28. Cf. GMN, 1991, 195.

29. GMN, 1991, 197.

30. Cf. also Elias *Plato's Defense of Poetry* (Albany: SUNY, 1984).

31. For an excellent feminist discussion of Aristotle's best tragedy, see Angela Curran, "Feminism and the Narrative Structures of the *Poetics*," in Cynthia Freeland, ed., *Feminist Interpretations of Aristotle* (University Park: Penn State, 1998).

32. John McCumber presents a wonderfully original "menstrual reading" of catharsis, suggesting that it is naturally linked with mimesis in the (male) spectator, who experiences catharsis, once he recognizes imitation qua imitation; catharsis is the intellectual "recognition that the spectacle is only a spectacle, an imitation and not reality, *is* its passing out of the body, as opposed to its absorption into a basis for action" (McCumber, 1988, 60).

33. Boal, *Theatre of the Oppressed* (London: Pluto Press, 1979), 34.

34. I want to draw attention to Marten's definition of poetics here, which expresses this non-Aristotelian aesthetic sentiment: "Poesie ist und bleibt ein Spiel, eine Inszenierung des Menschen, freilich ein Spiel voller Ernst und Realität. Das spielend-ernste Verhältnis zu Unendlichkeit und Unsterblichkeit ist ein Zeugnis poetischer Realität unter vielen, und damit eben ein Zeugnis von Realität," *Der menschliche Mensch: Abschied vom utopischen Denken* (Paderborn: Schöningh, 1988), 82.

35. Cf. Schiller (see also Chapter 4, below).

36. For an explanation of this term, cf. Marten, 1988.

37. McCumber, 1988, 61.

38. I am grateful to Angela Curran for a helpful discussion of the ontological shift of play in Aristotle.

39. Djuric notes Nietzsche's criticism of Aristotle for conceiving play as a lesser good, subordinated to higher life goals in M. Djuric, *Nietzsche und die Metaphysik* (Berlin, 1985), 176.

Chapter 4

PLAY OF THE ENLIGHTENMENT: KANT AND SCHILLER

Human life is not a game of joy but a concatenation of necessities and strenuous-ness [*Bemühungen*]. Only by being subjected to this constraint can we have en-joyment. Those who shun work, have to become savages or are overcome by boredom. They are afraid to die, because they have not felt life.
—Kant, *Reflexionen zur Anthropologie*, WW XV, 1104.

In the modern period we need to investigate in what ways the paidiophobic trends paved by Aristotle continue to effect Western thought and the legitimiza-tion or self-grounding desires within the modern discipline of philosophy.[1] I will leap over the medieval period, dominated by Catholic intellectual thought and indebted to Aristotelian philosophy.[2] What is novel in the Enlightenment era of Kant and Schiller is a different theorization of play, diverging from the Greek preoccupation with the play/seriousness dichotomy. With the rise of a bourgeois class and with the concomitant demise of feudalism, leisurely contemplation becomes somewhat democratized. More middle-class men and upper-class women engage in discussions of "l'art pour l'art" and debate the notion of lei-sure and how to spend one's pastime meaningfully. Philosophy in the age of the Enlightenment becomes compartmentalized (into epistemology, ethics, and aesthetics). Within the newly established field of aesthetics, we see a resurfacing of playful leisure—expressed in bourgeois art forms, for instance opera, drama, and literature.[3]

In this chapter, I shall pursue the malediction of play in Kant and Schiller's discussions of the concept and function of play. Although Kant, unlike Schiller, does not develop a play theory per se, nevertheless, he utilizes the concept enough so that one can rule out the possibility that Kant uses the "free play" of imagination as a mere "by-product" of its productive activity. Ingeborg Heide-mann's study (*Der Begriff des Spiels*, 1968) is the first of its kind which analy-ses play systematically in philosophical discourse. In his book *Einbildungskraft und Spiel* Andreas Heinrich Trebels (1967) focuses more specifically on the Kantian analysis of play and imagination. These studies have recently been am-plified by Makkreel's hermeneutic work *Imagination and Interpretation in Kant*

(1990). However, they do not give a historically situated analysis of Kant's play of the imagination nor a comparative approach, e.g., contrasting his conception with Hume's, Aquinas's, or Aristotle's play.[4] I will explore the Aristotelian thread of play in Kant's Critiques; in addition I will examine anthropological applications in the precritical work of "Observations on the Feeling of the Beautiful and Sublime" and in the postcritical work of *Anthropology from a Pragmatic Point of View*.[5]

Next, I will briefly discuss Friedrich Schiller, an avid reader of Kant's writings, whose work *On the Aesthetic Education of Man, in a Series of Letters* may not have great intrinsic philosophical value but had a considerable impact on Hegel and has shaped the way we think about aesthetics. Schiller, as Heidegger claims, has been the only one who "has grasped essential things vis-à-vis Kant's doctrine of the beautiful and of art."[6] In Schiller's writings, the purpose and the differentiation of play into ontological dichotomies is more pronounced than it is in Kant, since Schiller distinguishes explicitly between a transcendental play-drive and a material (psychophysiological) play-drive, giving primacy to the former—in good Kantian tradition. Notice that he echoes Aristotle's distinction, because he sets up his own dichotomy between the supreme play of the philosopher (qua *schole*, leisurely activity) and the mere pastimes of the many, who pursue material playthings.

Among philosophers it is commonly accepted that Schiller is influenced by Kant's radical subjectivism. This is evident in Schiller's own talk about players (and their games). With his emphatic benediction of play in the *Letters*, Schiller has inspired a generation of like-minded play theoreticians, such as Groos, Buytendijk, Huizinga, Bally, and Hartmann. Others, who have criticized Schiller's subjectivist approach, have developed a phenomenology of play (Scheuerl, Fink, and Gadamer).[7] In this chapter, we will trace the beginnings of subjectivist play. Both Kant and Schiller follow Aristotle's lead vis-à-vis play and its purposefulness and continue to disregard the Dionysian element of play.

Kant's Apollonian Ruminations on Play

First, we will turn to Kant's precritical period. In the essay "Beobachtungen über das Gefühl des Schönen und Erhabenen" (published in 1764, hereafter BSE), there are only five occurrences of the term "Spiel" and its composita (*Trauerspiel, Spielwerk*). Given the sparsity of occurrences, it does not seem important to give any attention to this essay, and in fact, this seems to be one of the reasons why many play theoreticians have chosen to ignore it. Play, however, surfaces here with a clearly social valorization. It is the means used to converse with women in public gatherings.[8] Male playfulness, i.e., demonstrating one's wit and cleverness, ("[seinen] munteren Witz spielen . . . lassen") at dinner table conversations is encouraged, according to Kant, in order to please women [*Frauenzimmer*], who embody the beautiful.[9] While women may also play in ways that demonstrate their wittiness, they are warned about transgressing (gendered) standards: a woman who is too witty, too precocious, is called a fool

(*Närrin*) (BSE A57). She is allowed to express only enough to show that she graciously welcomes any complements from the (sublime) male counterpart. Clearly, she may not venture far in her play, given the restrictions that are immediately placed on her. Kant's advice follows an infamous observation that he is doubtful that women ("the fair gender") are in fact capable of grasping first principles (A56). Kant goes as far as to declare that women are cast as the sexualized object of play, of the male gaze and wit, so that "[w]oman is always as woman a pleasant object of a well-behaved conversation" (A63). As subjugated players they all too willingly play along with male insinuations [*Anspielungen*], lest they be accused of being pedantic[10] or prudish. Kant claims that he merely opines on human behavior as an essayist, not as moral philosopher, because he "only" observes appearances, viz. feelings of the beautiful, and does not make moral judgments (A63). So, looking at the natives, as it were, our anthropologist makes armchair observations and gives pointers for correct behavior which somehow evade normative judgments.[11]

In French high society, good taste, or good playful conduct, is not exercised, according to Kant. First of all, necessary boundaries between jest and seriousness are shamelessly transgressed: "Important affairs are treated as jokes, and petty things get the most serious attention" (A90). One of those "petty things" is the *Frauenzimmer*.[12] But most disturbingly, in such conversations the other person becomes merely a toy [*Spielwerk*] for one's own pleasure, regardless of gender! While Kant has no objections to raise in his "empirical" discussions of how the "fair gender" is the play-object of dinner conversations in Prussian society, he is appalled by the social and political prominence of women in French (high) society. In a footnote he says that woman has the say at all parties: "Madame sets the tone." What is lost, Kant laments, is that woman is not truly honored in such a culture (A88-90).

There is a duplicitous tendency towards playfulness in this essay. Jesting and gallantry are expressly condoned, but "excesses" of play—especially in female jokers, or when play itself becomes a national pastime[13]—are a bad habit, an unfunny folly. The rules of the game are given by good taste (A57). Clearly, play has a specific function, if only to overcome the oppositional relation between the sexes ("Gegenverhältnis der Geschlechter") as required by bourgeois etiquette. In good Aristotelian tradition, Kant cautions against natural complementary boundaries; too much play is unbecoming of feminine behavior.

In pursuing the Aristotelian thread of "good" *schole* (leisure) vs. "bad" *paidia* (amusement), I contend that this oppositional couple has left its marks in this essay. The "fair sex" is differentiated when it comes to practices of play, seemingly incapable of enjoying clever games of the mind. Furthermore, playfulness has its *kairos*; if put to use in serious activities, these will inevitably become superficial, lightweight [*läppisch, leichtsinnig*] affairs.

In *The Critique of Pure Reason* (hereafter CPR), play is not valorized as a *different* kind of activity but as a negative activity. Kant repeatedly refers to the "mere" play of imagination [*Einbildungskraft*], which, according to him, has no import for the objective validity of empirical concepts. As Heidemann (1968) points out, "play is neither knowledge nor good in itself."[14] In the "Metaphysical

Deduction," Kant writes that synthesis is a rule-directed activity—"the act of putting different representations together, and of grasping what is manifold in them in one [act of] knowledge" (B103). The concepts (*Begriffe*) of the understanding which determine the way in which objects are thought do not impose any rule-governed constraint (*Zugriff*) to "mere" play of representations, which is a random, disorderly, spontaneous, subjective movement of the lower cognitive faculties (e.g., imagination). The study of speculative reason is a serious affair [*ein Geschäft*], a scientific endeavor, not a game of nonserious opining, which does not have the least bit in common, according to Kant, with the earnest search for truth (cf. the play of imagination in B850/A822). Kant often juxtaposes the opposites, *Geschäft* and *Spiel*, to ensure that caprice does not contaminate busywork (order and seriousness) in his transcendental analytic of concepts. Note, that Kant's *Spiel* is not a kind of *game*, where specific rules are introduced and followed by the players. The kind of play he refers to is lawless shifting trifle, a "playing with the cobwebs of the brain" (B196).

However, Kant makes room for play in transcendental dialectics (e.g., the dialectical play of cosmological ideas) (A462/B490). This kind of play (*Spielerei*, i.e., a play of fancy[15]) again does not submit itself to "the rules of experience." Such play is nothing more than mere illusion (*Schein*) or a false impression (*Blendwerk*); illusory play conjures up chimeras, unicorns but not determinable objects of experience. In this *Scheinwelt*, reason is unable to bring these cosmological ideas "into harmony" with truth, the laws of nature (A462/B490). Trebels suggests a positive use of play here, since illusion *is* the realm of truth within a game. Play has its own truth, its own reality.[16] Trebels seems to take to a Gadamerian interpretation of "good" play and—in a presentist move—imposes this reading on Kant's CPR. After all, Kant maintains that the speculative thinking of cosmological ideas yields meaninglessness [*Sinnleeres*, *Nonsens*] (A485/B513).[17] A play of representations does not satisfy the conditions required for knowledge, because it has nothing to do with rule-directed synthetic activities, which characterize pure concepts. I disagree with Menzer (1952), Trebels, and Heidemann, who loosely interpret the term "to put into play" [*ins Spiel setzen*] as Kant's way of introducing specific rules into the game of the critique of pure reason, which could suggest, misleadingly, that play has some epistemological significance in his critical methodology.

Let us turn to *The Critique of Practical Reason* (hereafter CPrR). Although there are only a few references to play, negative judgments about it abound. Kant vehemently argues against "a mere mechanical play" of contradictory pleasures (CPrR, p.68), i.e., where the moral agent finds himself at the whim of pleasures and pain.[18] Kant's deontological theory requires of the self to rely on the concept of duty, which follows the principles of pure practical reason (the moral law, autonomy of the good will). It is noteworthy that Kant frequently uses the expression *Widerspiel* (conflictual play, the back-and-forth movement, the subjective, fleeting, interplay of opposing affects) (cf. CPrR, 53, 61, 130). Heidemann points out correctly that the term *Widerspiel* is not synonymous with a logical contradiction.[19] It merely depicts the ephemeral, unreliable moral character of play (of passions).[20] Kant stresses that base pleasures are in *Widerspiel* to the feeling of respect for the moral law and hence have to be defeated (cf. CPrR, 130). In its moral application, free will is not playful; freedom here has nothing to do with "free play," which on the other hand is a key (positive) term in the aesthetic context of the third Critique.

Finally, *Urteilskraft* (the mental faculty of judgment) is condemned as a mere children's game, something practised only for competition's sake (CPrR, 275). Kant revises this "prejudgment" two years later with the publication of *The Critique of Judgment*, where he considers the aesthetic dimension of play. But this may be only prima facie a revisionist approach: Kant maligns play in the epistemological and ethical realm and approves play only in the aesthetic realm; thus the second Critique manifests his commitment to establishing semi-autonomous spheres of metaphysics, ethics, and aesthetics (and perhaps philosophical anthropology).

In both the first and second Critiques, play is held in contempt epistemologically, figuring as the Other of reason and understanding. "Mechanical" or haphazard play does not have a part in the second order rule-directed activities of pure concepts, which produce the synthetic unity of consciousness (cf. CPR A106). Is there a recognizable semantic shift of play in the third Critique?

In the *Critique of Judgment*, Kant attempts to recognize play's aesthetic function as interplay—not *Widerspiel*—of imagination and understanding. Yet, in this harmony of the faculties, play is not knowledge-producing either. However, the first part of the third Critique (which deals solely with a critique of taste) features new aspects of play which have influenced later play theoreticians (notably Schiller). Where *The Critique of Practical Reason* ridicules the play of judgment as mere child's play and *The Critique of Pure Reason* discounts any serious critical study of aesthetics, Kant commits a ludic turn in his third Critique where he probes judgments of taste and holds that they are indeed synthetic judgments a priori.

In recent years it has been fashionable to break with those aestheticians who criticize Kant's *Critique of Judgment* (KdU)[21] as shallow and subjectivist. Trebels (1967) and Makkreel (1990) argue for a complete reevaluation of the third Critique and assail Gadamer's standpoint for his dismissal of Kant's aesthetics as subjectivist.[22] Kemal (1992) criticizes those who chide Kant for introducing a formalist aesthetic theory (notably Crawford 1974). On the other hand, defenders of Gadamer's view maintain that Kant prejudges, if not, maligns, play when he talks about *das bloße Spiel* of the imagination (e.g., Heidemann 1968).[23] Kant's subjectivism and his elevation of genius make possible a novel kind of play—one that breaks free from traditional Aristotelian aesthetic standards, which lays out specific rules for the manner of imitating great works of art, such as tragedy. Kant maintains that aesthetic judgments which have universal validity are communicable.[24] Yet Kant cannot bring himself to part completely with Aristotle. In both *The Critique of Judgment* and in the *Anthropology* Kant again displays Aristotelian tendencies insofar as he describes a playful activity as "the Other" of seriousness; play, for instance, a conversation, may not have a purpose, except that it is enjoyable in itself. It may also serve as relaxation.[25] In Kant play is simply a pleasurable activity, in an aesthetic—not pathological—sense! Kant says that play is something that is *an sich angenehm*. Yet, Kant's nse! Kant says that play is something that is *an sich angenehm*. Yet, Kant's use of the term *Spiel* is quite ambiguous in the third Critique; in some instances it is (positively) identified with the aesthetic judgment, which mediates between Reason and understanding. In the section on the "Analytic of the Sublime" (KdU, §§23), however, Kant turns against play—so to speak—by stating that this feeling is "no play but seriousness . . ." (KdU, 75)—which is consistent with his precritical reflection on the sublime and beautiful.

In exploring the meanings (and tensions) of Kant's play in the KdU, I want to put forth the following leading questions: (1) What is the function of imagination in KdU? How is it used in the first as compared with the third Critique? (2) What is free play, rule-directed play, and what is the significance of examples? (3) What is the role of free play vis-à-vis aesthetic pleasure?

(1) There is much disagreement about the interpretation of the function of play, which is so intricately tied to the faculty of imagination. In order to make sense of the interconnection, "harmonious interplay" between imagination and understanding, we will first have to understand the role of imagination in the first and third Critiques.

Makkreel's study suggests that a reevaluation of imagination [*Einbildungskraft*] takes place in Kant's first Critique. Kant follows Leibniz, Baumgarten, and Wolff in arguing against the Cartesian dismissal of imagination as an arbitrary sensory power and prone to give false judgment.[26] What is novel in Kant's first Critique is that he assigns a double function to imagination, i.e., imagination is both a productive and a merely reproductive mental activity. Insofar as this cognitive faculty is able to conjure up images creatively and spontaneously, it is a transcendental a priori faculty, synthesizing inner sense prior to all experience; in its reproductive capacity, imagination merely replicates objects empirically (a posteriori), i.e., according to empirical laws that it does not conceptualize.[27] Kant notes famously that the synthesizing activity of the imagination is "a blind but indispensible function of the soul without which we should have no knowledge whatsoever, but of the existence of which we are scarcely ever conscious" (CPR A78/B103). We have to ask at this point: does this double function of imagination "carry over" to the third Critique and, more importantly, does its synthesizing activity remain, as it were, at the preconscious level?

Henrich (1992) claims that the third Critique is more precise than the first Critique in describing the employment of the harmonious play of mental faculties and in presenting a new aesthetic theory about the relationship between understanding and imagination, feeling and play.[28] However, Kant remains vague in his description of the structure of "harmonious play." Trebels, on the other hand, maintains that the role of imagination and its play (with understanding) is not remarkably different in the two Critiques. Trebels's analysis is provocative and original yet rather "imaginatively" interprets Kant's aesthetic theory, as a coherent one, even though Trebels notes that *The Critique of Pure Reason* rejects the possibility of a philosophical theory of aesthetics (cf. CPR, B35n.). Trebels claims that the first Critique has to be considered foundational for the critique of aesthetic judgment.[29] I agree with his claim; however, I find it doubtful that there is no interpretive shift with respect to the function of imagination, once Kant was determined to write a book about an aesthetic theory that makes universal validity claims about judgments of taste which do not rely on rational proof or experience.

Makkreel also counters Trebels's position by stating that he does not account for the different function of imagination in the third Critique, a function quite dissimilar from its synthesizing activity in the first Critique. Makkreel notes how odd it is that it is so frequently overlooked that Kant says nothing of the faculty of intuition and its crucial function in the synthesis of apprehension in the KdU. Makkreel argues with Trebels that it is imprecise to reduce "felt harmony" to "synthesis," since the former is a reciprocal relation that brings about attunement between two elements (imagination and understanding) and the latter is a one-sided influence "for the sake of strict unity."[30] It is therefore plausible to note a revaluation of imagination in the third Critique. However, it seems that imagination still has subservient "immature" status; that is, imagination faces the disciplinary straitjacket of understanding. To make sense of this disciplinary effect, we will need to take into account the role of play, particularly, free play.

(2) Play is intricately intertwined with imagination in the first and third Critiques. Prima facie, there is an important shift from "mere" play (indicating its derivative role) to the "free" (authentic?) play of imagination (and understanding).

Free play in the KdU is spontaneous, lively, voluntary, not bound by law or concepts. Imagination is free—insofar as it rejects all rigid regularity—and at the same time is productive in accordance with the law without following the law: "[a]nything that gives the imagination scope for unstudied and final [zweckmäßig] play is always fresh to us. We do not grow to hate the very sight of it" (§22, 73). Without being subservient to the synthesizing, unifying activity of understanding, imagination plays within the *Spielraum* mandated by this higher cognitive faculty. Barriers are imposed on the play of imagination through the unifying drive of understanding, as Gadamer puts it.[31] However, these barriers do not present an obstacle, merely a demarcation of sorts in order to make play possible. Kant allows for a self-determining role of imagination—a freedom from external, imposed rules.[32] Kant's genius creates artistic forms which become the standard. He produces the artwork in isolation. This represents a decisive shift from the Aristotelian organic development of paradigmatic art—epitomized by Sophoclean tragedies—to provide guidelines for what constitutes good play. The creative play of imagination is a key concept of the modern individualist worldview which is opposed to the ancient organic worldview.[33] The enlightened creator of artworks is celebrated as a heretic, as a true originator of his work. He does not copy traditional aesthetic ideas but is licensed to radically depart from it. Traditional and community standards have no longer a binding aesthetic force.

Nevertheless, Kant's discussion of play (of the imagination) is still indebted to Aristotle. Play has no significant epistemological role in Kant. Good play is an activity which is engaged with disinterested interest, with affects that are free from pathological desires (e.g., obsessions with chance-games). But Kant insists that the free play of imagination is merely concerned with objects of beauty (such play is goal-free), to be differentiated from lively, goal-oriented games of music, chance-play, and jest; the purpose of wit, for instance, consists in contributing to good health of the body.[34]

How then does Kant make sense of the problem of "free" play and of a game played according to rules? What kind of play is *mise-en-scène*? In the introduction to the KdU, Kant rejects a mere psychological solution to the problem of the generalizability of judgments of taste, since that methodology is unable to determine "according to which rule our cognitive faculties really carry out their game [=*ihr Spiel wirklich treiben*]" (KdU, xxxi). What is needed is a transcendental deduction of judgments of taste, and that is exactly what Kant is determined to show. The lengthy deduction of pure aesthetic judgments (§§30-54) introduces the notion of the genius. Kant then reveals that the genius is capable of prescribing rules for fine art. In judging a beautiful object, the genius grasps spontaneously the fast, free flowing, ephemeral play of imagination.

In the act of aesthetic cognition, imagination and understanding play in accord; in other words, they are in tune with each other. Makkreel notes that "[i]t is the accord necessary for all cognition that is appealed to in the deduction of taste to assure that aesthetic judgments are universal."[35] But he also criticizes a hasty conflation of attunement or harmony with synthesis, the latter being a necessary unifying act initiated by one faculty only, namely understanding. Harmony, on the other hand, is a "reciprocal relation between two distinct elements,"[36] and Kant's insistence that this harmony must be the result of a noncoerced interaction between the two cognitive faculties seems to substantiate Makkreel's claim.

If this distinction is to be upheld, what is one to make of synthetic judgments of taste? Makkreel ascertains that "synthetic" here is to be qualified as merely "synthetic in form," pertaining to the subjective state of mind.[37] Suppose Kant has such a distinct use of the term "synthesis" in mind, does that mean that aesthetic synthesizing is an activity performed according to a rule? But that would involve a concept, i.e., a universal which serves as a rule (cf. CPR). Kant however explicitly denies that concepts are "put into play" in the KdU. After all, the cognitive faculties are engaged in a free play, "because no definite concept restricts them to a particular rule of cognition" (§9, 28).[38] Imagination is a cognitive faculty which conjures up fantasies, perceptions, or thoughts without being subdued by—or subservient to—understanding's synthesis.

It is perplexing—as Henrich has noted—that Kant neglects (or perhaps he purposefully toys with us?) to specify the structure of the play, in particular with respect to the interplay of imagination and understanding. Henrich (1992) speculates that Kant can only have in mind a harmonious play "between imagination in its freedom and understanding in its lawfulness."[39] This interplay is characterized positively as lively [*erleichtert*], literally, relieved; here *erleichtert* carries the meaning of being nonreflective, carefree, perhaps displaying Kant's interest in Rococo aesthetics: "in the more facile play [*im erleichterten Spiele*] of both mental powers (imagination and understanding) as quickened [*belebt*] by their mutual accord" (§9, 31). It is a unanimous sentiment [*einhellig*], a subjective, self-sustaining and enlivened movement of *Geist*—actualized or set in motion by the genius—which "sets the mental powers into a swing that is final, i.e., into a play which is self-maintaining and which strengthens those powers for such activity" (§49). These attributes seem to suggest a more or less chaotic, uncontrollable back and forth movement of playful interaction that dominates the aesthetic field of taste.

However, it is not the case that Kant conjures up Bacchic frenzy. Rather, one should be thinking of an orderly baroque minuet dancing formation. Kant says that the play of aesthetic impressions (perceptions of sound and color) is "orderly" [*regelmässig*] (§14, 40); but he qualifies that statement by suggesting that "orderliness" [*Regelmässigkeit*] should be avoided if it is accompanied by coercion (§23, 71). Yet, restrictions apply, since freedom (of associations) in playful fancy is to be represented as "being subjected to a lawful business [*gesetzliches Geschäft*]" (116). Jane Kneller goes further to argue that imagination is still cast as an immature faculty and a junior partner to understanding: "Imagination in judgments of taste resembles far more a docile schoolchild let out to play, with the understanding in the background nodding approval at her antics, and keeping a watchful eye lest she attempt to leave the school yard."[40]

Kant denies that the interplay or *Widerspiel* of affects has anything to do with the dominance of understanding, with intellectualism; on the other hand, as Kneller points out, he does not rule out certain "lawful" constraints in this *Spielraum*. After all, how can the faculties of understanding and imagination interact harmoniously if imagination does not act in conformity to the law? Henrich (1992) maintains that the upshot of Kant's formalistic theory on imagination and understanding is to draw a clear distinction between an ontological/mathematical form and an aesthetic form.[41] This would suggest differentiating the meanings of play with respect to an intellectual and a sensory realm. Thus play is maligned in the first and second Critiques (as "mere play") and validated (as "free play") in the third Critique, which is concerned with pure aesthetic judgments. Hence it is wrong to argue that play has the same meaning throughout Kant's work.[42] Even though abstract play seems to lack cognition in both Critiques, one has to look at the shifts of meaning. There is a decidedly affirmative perspective on play in the third Critique, yet it has an increasingly intellectual (and instrumental) tendency, even though this is disavowed in the discussion of pleasure. (See below.)

The problem of intellectualism is foregrounded when Kant notes that play is a rule-directed activity in his analysis of the role of *examples* in the KdU.[43] An example is the place holder for a certain objective rule. In §18, there is a noteworthy emphasis on "exemplary" judgments. Kant indicates that the modality of judgments of taste is not of logical necessity but of a necessity of a special kind: "it is a necessity of everyone's endorsement of a singular judgment, which is to be regarded as an example of a general rule, which cannot be named" (62-63). Hence, examples mysteriously hint at "general rules," since reflective judgment (of taste) is not equipped with concepts, i.e., universal principles which serve as rules (cf. CPR, A95-97). In §59, examples are defined as empirical concepts, being opposed to schemata, i.e., pure concepts of understanding (KdU, 254).

Poetry, for instance, often uses examples of experience (i.e., death, jealousy, vices) (§49, 194). Poets also play with illusions [*Schein*] which are beyond any experience (§53). Kant approves of their deceptive game, since they promise little with their "mere play of ideas" and infuse life into concepts through productive imagination. There is a familiar Aristotelian ring to this assertion, for the suggestion that possibility (within the play world of fantasies) pleases aesthetically more than mere reality (play with concepts of experience).

In §14, entitled "Exemplifications," Kant lays out a formalistic definition of play on the varieties of judgments of taste, which has puzzled many Kant scholars. He states:

> All form of objects of sense (both of external and also, mediately, of internal sense) is either *figure* or *play*: in the latter case, it is either play of figures (in space: mimic and dance) or mere play of sensations (in time). (42)

Inner sense, as we know from the first Critique, is the subjective time order, whereas outer sense refers to the category of space. Inner sense is mediated through the free play of imagination (cf. schematism in CPR). Outer sense is not involved in the interplay of imagination and understanding, which is the condition for common sense (KdU, §20). Trebels maintains that, because play appears here as shape [*Gestalt, Gebilde*], this formalistic definition of play is Kant's attempt to consider the problem of an objective conception of play.[44] In fact, this definition stands out in the KdU insofar as Kant does not mention play as *Gestalt* again, except in two instances: first, it appears negatively in the description of the sublime as "shape-less," and secondly, it appears in connection with "many games," that is, fine arts (poetry, painting, and music). Painting, Kant says, depends on external sensory impressions (§51, 205).[45] In fine art, however, the subjectivist interpretation prevails due to the dominant role of the genius, who displaces the generic critic (of good taste). Interestingly, Kant invokes a peculiar *Verbot* of mimesis. The genius's work of art is supposed to be a sample, "i.e., exemplary and should not originate from imitation" (§46, 182). This is a truly modern conception of the artist, who is allowed to defy all traditional norms and asked to set new standards and to determine aesthetic rules.

But is the genius's exemplary taste able to adjudicate the sublime—in a playful way? Kant is uneasy about answering this question. He suggests that, since the sublime is characterized by a feeling of displeasure, it has nothing to do with play, but "seems to be" (note Kant's cautiousness!) a serious, as opposed to playful, stimulating emotion, an activity of imagination (§23, 75). The feeling of the sublime is a feeling of dis-pleasure [*Unlust*] which lacks the life-affirming sensations that a playful imagination generates. Deleuze (1994) states that the harmony among the faculties is deceptive; instead, what Kant's analytic of the sublime reveals is violence, dissemblance, and phantasm:

> It is not the gods which we encounter: even hidden, the gods are only the forms of recognition. What we encounter are the demons, the sign-bearers: powers of the leap, the interval, the intensive and the instant; powers which only cover difference with more difference. What is most important, however, is that—between

sensibility and understanding, between imagination and memory, between memory and thought—when each disjointed faculty communicates to another the violence which carries it to its own limit, every time it is a free form of difference which awakens the faculty, and awakens it as the different within that difference.[46]

In the third Critique, Kant plays out the harmonious interaction between imagination and understanding (with respect to the Beautiful) against the discordant, cacophonous, even violent interplay between imagination and understanding (with respect to the Sublime) (KdU, §27). What this signals is the hidden agonistic aspect in the Apollonian, "outed" by Heidegger's discussion of the hermeneutic circle in *Being and Time* with respect to the Notion or Concept (*Begriff*).[47] *Begreifen* is the violent act of ordering or grasping the sensible, imagined manifold in Thought or Reason. Kant's emphasis on harmonious play should not mislead us into authenticating it as such. As Deleuze notes, "the harmony between the faculties can appear only in the form of a *discordant harmony*, since each communicates to the other only the violence which confronts it with its own difference and it divergence from the others."[48] Nietzsche, therefore, is wrong to impute that both orderliness *and* nonagonism appear in Apollonian play (e.g., in the concept of *principium individuationis*); he simply goes along with Kant's "pretend-play" of putative harmony between the faculties, which only clash with respect to the sublime.[49]

While Kant presents a challenge in determining the role of abstract play in his critique of taste, it is clear that the genius has a decisive role to play vis-à-vis the special case of fine art, not only as arbiter but also as producer of beautiful artworks. In the case of fine art, Kant sets up a hierarchy by ranking poetry above all other works of art, and music as least pleasing, since it "merely plays with emotions" and lacks a certain "urbanity" (KdU, §53, pp.220-21).[50] All other "higher" forms of art at least play appropriately with imagination *and* understanding so that their work is not completely without *raison* (220). Here we see an invocation of a play, an intellectual game of sorts that also deserves to be labelled "Apollonian." As we shall see this has consequences for the role of play with respect to aesthetic pleasure.

(3) In the context of judgments of taste, pleasure (*Lust*) is defined as being an aesthetic affect, lacking pathological or intellectual tendencies, or as Gadamer puts it, "being free from sensualist and rationalist prejudices."[51] A proper pleasurable experience of the beautiful merely is disinterested sentiment. The subject's feeling of pleasure stems from a formal (i.e., subjective) purposefulness which is to be found "in the play of the cognitive faculties of the Subject" (§12, 36-37). Here it seems that Kant is really toying with us, making us believe that such pleasure is purely aesthetically motivated. Kant's pietist critique of taste clearly is marked by an intellectualism, especially since Kant strives to show that such judgments are indeed universal, i.e., to be approved by everybody.[52] Free play (of fancy) is only free insofar as it does not go beyond the normative boundaries which are posited by understanding.

In §54 there is another instance of how Kant imagines the link between play and feelings of pleasure: "All changing free play of affects (which are not based

on any intentions) gives pleasure" (223; my translation). Employing a formalistic invocation of purposefulness without a purpose, playfulness serves here as a
means to improve one's well-being; play, e.g., telling jokes, laughter, which is
the comic effect of the metamorphosis of "a strained expectation being suddenly
reduced into nothing," brings about balance of vital forces and a feeling of
healthiness in the body (p.225).[53] In other words, a playful wit improves diges-
tion and thus has a cleansing effect.[54] Playful activities, such as entertaining
evening parties (a favorite example in Kant's anthropological treatises), "must
be pleasurable," Kant says in an almost chatty tone, for "without play they
hardly ever escape falling flat" (§54; cf. *Anthropology* 1974, §88).

While Kant's *Critique of Judgment* clearly shows signs of his flirtation with
the Rococo,[55] his philosophical commitment portrays play as ideologically suspect, as that which is too carefree and therefore may not be adequately tamed (as
the failure of music shows). Even as Kant emphatically holds that play is free,
not logically constrained, in aesthetic judgments, he seems to prefer play to be
constrained by rules of understanding. In his aesthetical writings play is not depicted as carefree, chaotic, Bacchanalian (Dionysian), but it is always somehow
in conformity with the law (qua *Spielregeln*). Hence, Apollonian, intellectual
values not only dominate but do so at the expense of the Dionysian. Nevertheless, Kant sees possibilities for the social value of play in aesthetic judgments.
Play seems useful and almost able to enter the realm of the sublime. Furthermore, the genius's free play of the faculty of imagination spontaneously creates
new standards of beauty and disavows mimetic representations.

Anthropology From a Pragmatic Point of View (hereafter, *Anthropology*),
Kant's postcritical work first published in 1797, focuses on using empirical rules
to describe human behavior and on using other persons skillfully (i.e., pragmati-
cally) for one's own purposes.[56] In this context, Kant reflects on acceptable and
unacceptable masks of playing, toying with others, i.e., a play which is illusion-
ary, artificial, and deceptive.

In the section "On Artificial Play with Sensory Semblance," he approves of
an acceptable, i.e., natural, play of illusions which is "the kind of false impression that persists even though we know that the supposed object is not real"
(§13, 149). This type of impression is held up against an artificial, i.e., a deceptive or fraudulent, play of the senses, e.g., conjuring tricks, where the distinction
between fact and fiction is blurred. His poignant example to contrast the two
different types: the color of a dress that makes a face beautiful is a seductive
illusion, but donning makeup is fraud, a bad hoax (150). Kant has the urge to
navigate through the troubling morass of sensory appearance, giving his nod to
play that pretends to be portraying reality, but where "we" know fully well it
isn't, and dismissing play that doesn't stick to its realm of fiction but transgresses it. He makes a similar point in KdU, when he contrasts poetry and rhetoric. Poetry is honest "business," whereas rhetoric as the art of persuasion is deceptive (cf. KdU §53).

If we haven't already noticed an underlying moralizing attitude in his
evaluation of play, Kant is more heavy-handed—and Aristotelian—in the section "On Permissable Moral Semblance," which discusses the limits of roles a

moral agent can enact (§14). Kant finds it acceptable play-acting when one is duped by another's fake friendliness (in the hope that they might become serious and develop that virtue out of enacting it) and this is also permissable if we dupe ourselves: " . . . to deceive the deceiver within ourselves, inclination, is to return to obeying the law of virtue; it is not a deception, but an innocent [*rühmliche*] illusion of ourselves" (§14, 151). Yet, he also holds that the mere moral semblance rather than the genuine presence of the good in the self cannot be tolerated, for it is moral self-deception and leads to making excuses for one's behavior (§14, 153). Note again the oppositional pairing of the play of pretending and virtuous seriousness. While Kant does not consider role-playing inherently bad, not knowing when to throw away the mask (the veil of deception), he thinks, is despicable.

Here we find an interesting depiction of play, akin to Aristotle's *schole*. A leisurely game is purposeless in itself, which, for instance, is true of a "peaceful struggle" of a game inspired by the fine arts or conversation; nevertheless it is more than just "killing time" because "we are at least cultivating our mind" (152).

In §31 ("On the Constructive Power Belonging to Sensibility [*sinnliches Dichtungsvermögen*]") Kant revisits the various functions of the imagination. It is noteworthy that, in illustrating its uses, he also notes proper and improper applications. Kant says in jest that "[w]e like to play with our imagination, and often do it; but imagination (in its role of fantasy) plays with us just as often, and sometimes most inopportunely" (175). Its play obviously needs to be disciplined, i.e., bound by rules, especially in conversations, which deteriorate when people simply spout out their free associations on any given topic (177; cf. §47). Thus, the free play of imagination ought to be (blindly) in conformity with laws [*gesetzmäßig*] without being constrained by understanding (cf. KdU's argumentation).

In my analysis of Kant's play theory I have attempted to probe the question of whether play is connected with rules or is simply something irrational and entirely subjective. In the aesthetic realm, the free play of imagination and understanding is the condition of the possibility of judging beautiful objects and setting new standards of art. Its free activity is purposeful, yet it does not aim at a purpose; thus Kant emphasizes a nonutilitarian aspect of play, which has great importance for Schiller's writings on aesthetic education. However, Kant retains Aristotle's characterization of the ontological and epistemological status of play by noting that metaphysical discussions after all are not supposed to be mere *Spielwerk* (cf. *Prolegomena*, WWIV, 369). Just as Gadamer (1986a) chides Kant for ignoring the truth claim within art (its *Wahrheitsanspruch*), one can criticize Kant for being ambivalent toward play in the context of the sublime. However, Kant's approach towards play within the aesthetic realm differs from Aristotle's approach towards leisurely contemplation, which is serious business not subjected to any unregulated, inopportune, seductive lure. Kant also breaks with Aristotle by establishing the semiautonomous disciplines of metaphysics, ethics, and aesthetics (where the latter borders on applications in philosophical anthropology). While Kant certainly is not as dismissive of play's cognitive potential

as is Aristotle, clearly his game is Apollonian in character; Bacchanalian skir-
mishes of the imagination are too unruly to be considered, since they would ex-
plode the neat, orderly boundaries of his Prussian aesthetic *Spielraum*.

Schiller's Theory of Play Impulses

Schiller, who is clearly under Kant's aesthetic spell, nevertheless de-emphasizes
the role of taste and common sense and instead elevates the role of the genius.
Schiller departs from the Kantian and Aristotelian tradition and yet remains
chained to them, exemplified in his theoretical writings, *On the Aesthetic Education of Man, in a Series of Letters* and *On Grace and Dignity*.

Schiller's major philosophical work *On Grace and Dignity* ("Über Anmut
und Würde," written in 1793; hereafter AuW) reveals his close reading of
Kant's third Critique and is his first major attempt at formulating a theory of
play. According to him, play has a subjective component; play is not play of the
world (Fink) but always relates to players. It is the function of the person, "the
free principle within," which determines the play of appearances (AuW, 263).
The main player Schiller has in mind is of course the genius. As a supreme
product of nature, he produces beautiful works of art and sets new standards "by
accelerating the game" (AuW, 275). What is fashionable tomorrow is created by
the playful, spontaneous genius today. Schiller displaces Kant's critique of taste
(which is generalizable) and elevates the genius to prescribe *la mode* and to
make it accessible to the many, who are free to imitate the product. Yet, Schiller's conception of the genius follows Kant insofar as, due to the genius's natural talents, he creates things playfully—an ability which is "more admired than
an acquired ability of the spirit" (AuW, 275). In the KdU, Kant notes that the
genius's inspirations are original and not dependent on acquired taste or knowledge.

What is also novel in Schiller's theory is that the "beauty of play" takes
precedence over Kantian "free play" (AuW, 264; 279). Moreover, Schiller defines beautiful play as the interplay of reason and sensibility (282). Thus reason
plays a decisive part in defining the beauty of play, even though it may come
into "the business" of judgment belatedly—the process of a hermeneutic delay,
so to speak (264). As Sdun argues, the concept of play is subordinated to that of
freedom in AuW, a relationship whose valence is reversed in the fully developed
play theory of the *Letters* (cf.19th letter).[57] In the essay (AuW) freedom refers
to the "free principle" in the self, a rational, self-conscious autonomous agent
(cf. AuW, 263).   Nevertheless, Schiller, as a romantic poet, emphasizes the
beauty of play in order to "soften" Kantian deontology—and he poses the following question to the moral philosopher: "Just because the moral wimp wants
to give the law of reason a *laxness*, which makes it a play-thing [*Spielwerk*] of
his convenience, did it have to get a *rigidity*, which could only serve to trans-
form the most powerful expression of moral freedom into a more laudable form
of servitude?" (AuW, 285) Schiller's own (playful) solution is more fully developed in the *Letters*, as we will see below: the free, i.e., rational self is down-

played and the concept of freedom is captured by the expression of the "mixed nature" of the aesthetic and physical impulses in the self.

In his *On the Aesthetic Education of Man, in a Series of Letters* (hereafter, *Letters*), Schiller admits being indebted to "Kantian principles," on which his elaborations are based (*Letters*, 1, 309). But far from merely parroting Kant's methodology, he puts forth an original play theory by utilizing the terms, *Formtrieb* and *Stofftrieb*, which he considers fundamental drives in humans (12, 344). The play-drive is the composite of these drives, it is not a fundamental element itself (12, 347). It has to be "cultivated" in aesthetic education.[58] Hence it is wrong for Huizinga (1950) and Jünger (1953) to suggest, as Sdun (1966) points out, that play-drive has anything to do with an "innate drive." Sdun says that "drive" has a broader meaning than indicated by modern psychology.[59]

In the famous fifteenth letter, Schiller gives new meaning to neutralism by claiming that his theory of *Spieltrieb* is an impulse which is neither subjectively nor objectively contingent, yet neither externally nor internally necessary (15, 357). This observation leads him to contest the role of "mere" play and says that it is in fact only through play that humans are fully developed in their humanity. He postulates: " . . . humans only play when they are in the fullest sense of the word human beings, and they are only fully human beings when they play."[60] Despite this emphatic proclamation of "fully human human beings,"[61] Schiller does not discard the dichotomies of work and play, of reason and sense perception;[62] furthermore, he ranks an ideal or "transcendent" play-drive over a mere material or physical play-drive (cf. 27th letter).

Gadamer also holds Schiller responsible for separating "aesthetics" from its original meaning of perception and introducing the moral value of taste.[63] As Gadamer sums matters up, Schiller's postulate in the letters is: "Comport yourself aesthetically!"[64] Yet, despite the fact that a playful attitude is an intrinsic part of the (moral) self, it seems odd that Schiller still clings to the Kantian conception of the play-seriousness dichotomy, e.g., in contrasting play and "seriousness of principles" (*Letters* 9, 336; 22, 380). He also relies on Kant's distinction between the sublime and the beautiful by juxtaposing grace and play—as expression of the beautiful—with dignity and seriousness, where the latter pair gains importance vis-à-vis moral actions and the feeling of the sublime (AuW, 208). On the other hand, Schiller argues that it is only through play with beauty that the self gains "completion" (15, 358) and that play in art leads to a beneficial influence on the moral self ("On the Cause of Pleasure," in *Werke*, 135).

However, not all playful activity is equally valued. As we have seen with respect to a hierarchy in drives (formal and material), physical play is deemed inferior to aesthetic play:

So nature gives a pre-play of the unlimited in its material realm, and thus she already picks up the constraints *in part*, which she will discard completely in the realm of form. From the coercion of necessities or of *physical seriousness* she moves toward the aesthetic play—beyond the coercion of superfluity or of *physical play.*" (*Letters* 25, 406; Schiller's emphasis)[65]

Note that aesthetic play as a higher kind of play is akin to Aristotle's philosopher's leisurely contemplation. In fact, it is an intellectualist (Apollonian) play that Schiller comes to value in the aesthetic education of the self. The letters are written at the time of the French Revolution; and the subordination of animalistic play is probably Schiller's response to the horrors of the Jacobins' terror. This could perhaps explain why material (Dionysian) drives serve as the "abject"[66] in Schiller's aesthetic writings. Trebels (who does not take the historical situation into account) assesses these conflictual impulses (Apollonian and Dionysian) differently; he notes that reconciliation (*Versöhnung*) figures as a key motif in Schiller's play theory. The play-impulse synthesizes oppositional drives in humans: "For Schiller, the authentic being of humans finds its fulfillment in play. Here the self's unity is reestablished, the unity of sensibility and reason, of inclination and duty . . . of material and formal impulses."[67]

Trebels suggests that aesthetic judgment gains a mediating role for Schiller. In aesthetic play a sublation between the opposite faculties of reason and sensibility takes place so that the subject's "double nature" is reconciled.[68] But Trebels does not comment on the hierarchy of "games" Schiller sets up; in my mind, reconciliation does not amount to a dynamic movement between equally valued principles. Such reconciliation is a mere "partial" union, which is fleeting in character, because it merely offers a temporary retreat into the aesthetic play dimension which is separate and distinct from real (material) life experience. The material side seems to be temporarily suspended in this union.[69]

I will now turn to the sociopolitical implications of Schiller's play theory. What kind of society does he imagine where such play could thrive? In the last letter (27th), Schiller conjures up an ideal state, which is aesthetic in character and imbued with certain political demands of the French Revolution (foremost, equality) and philosophical ideals of the Enlightenment. In Schiller's aesthetic state, the self's realization of pleasure improves qualitatively (*veredelt*), e.g., by breaking out of the circle of brute obsession (*so ist sein thierischer Kreis aufgethan*); beyond mere material satisfaction akin to animalistic play (27, 405). To enter this "beyond" imagination one has to make a decisive leap and freely submit to the legislative force of understanding: "in this state, for the first time legislative spirit mingles with the actions of a blind instinct and subjects [*unterwirft*] the voluntary doings of imagination to spirit's unchanging eternal unity, putting its autonomy into the changing element and its infinity into the sensible element" (27, 407). Reason is not required to make playful leaps here. In fact, that would constitute another path only to be walked by free spirits. Women, subaltern subjects, of course, do not have such lofty aspirations, since they have been depicted as hardly capable of articulating their rational, non-brutish side.

Concluding, I want to suggest that Schiller's conception of an aesthetic state, in which humans ought to comport themselves playfully, certainly has potentiality to break out of the ludic malediction that has been prescribed by Aristotle; however, this ideal state offers only fleeting metaphysical comfort. As Gadamer puts it: "The freedom of the soul . . . is freedom merely in an aesthetic state and not in reality."[70] Schiller does not give up the dualism of aesthetic play possibilities and material necessities and thus remains indebted to the Aristotelian dichotomous conception of leisure (for the few and gifted) and play (for the many and brutishly inclined).

Schiller's emphatic engagement with play seems to clash with the claim that he, too, practices a malediction of play. Yet, I contend that the valorization of a certain kind of play (in fact, ideal play) makes him prone to reject play which is not in accord, indeed, collides, with this ideal. Hence, as we noticed in Aristotle, both Kant and Schiller reassert the importance of the irreconcilable differentiation between playful and serious affairs, each having its *kairos*, to be sure, but they cannot condone the intermingling of the two. It is Hegel who finally breaks out of casting play as the Other in philosophical discourse and Nietzsche who completes the ludic turn by fully casting the notion of *menschlicher Mensch* as *spielender Mensch* without engaging in a malediction of either term.

Notes

1. Andrew Cutrofello provides a suggestive analysis in claiming that Kant originates the conception of philosophy as a "discipline," heretofore thought of as a "faculty" in *Discipline and Critique. Kant, Postructuralism and the Problem of Resistance* (Albany: SUNY, 1994), 116.

2. Other marginalized intellectual trends are worth looking at for a sustained analysis of their discussion of play. While the Catholic intellectual tradition furthered Aristotle's malediction of Dionysian play, Kabbalistic and Christian mystics, such as Mechthild von Magdeburg, toy with "irrational aspects of Reason and therefore validate a deviant kind of playfulness. Irrationality, or better a-rationality, is akin to play, because, it falls in the realm of abjectionable thinking "stuff," producing—in the language of the metaphysicians—nonserious, nondemonstrable, and superficial trifle, i.e., the very things commonly associated with play.

3. In Georg Lukács's eyes, the bourgeois historical novel suffers from the rise of social Darwinism—its perversions and ahistoricity is exemplified in Malthus's ideology and Nietzsche's mythical yearnings. "Capitalist competition is swollen into a metaphysical history-dissolving mystique by the 'eternal law' of the struggle for existence. The most telling historical conception of this kind is the philosophy of Nietzsche, which makes a composite mythology out of Darwinism and the Greek contest, Agon" (*The Historical Novel* [New York: Humanities Press, 1965], 175).

4. Makkreel does however historicize imagination, viz. the importance it gained in post-Cartesian German thought (see below).

5. My analysis of *The Critique of Pure Reason* is indebted to Robert Paul Wolff's *Kant's Theory of Mental Activity* (Cambridge: Harvard University, 1963) and his Kant seminar (Spring 1989).

6. Martin Heidegger, *Nietzsche* Vol. I (Pfullingen), 137.

7. I am adopting here Trebels's analysis, who follows Heidemann in this categorization of the divergent play tendencies (Trebels, *Einbildungskraft und Spiel: Untersuchungen zur Kantischen Ästhetik, Kantstudien-Ergänzungshefte*, 93 [Bonn: Bouvier, 1967], 210).

8. Note a parallel to the third Critique, *The Critique of Judgment*, where the reference to women is dropped, but where play is relevant in determining a beautiful object yet irrelevant in determining a sublime object (cf. also *Anthropology*, 277-78).

9. "Die Tugend des Frauenzimmers ist eine schöne Tugend. Die des männlichen Geschlechts soll eine edele Tugend sein. Sie [i.e., *women*] werden das Böse vermeiden,

nicht weil es unrecht sondern weil es häßlich ist." (A55-56).

10. Kant uses the peculiar term "Ehrbarkeitspedantin" in this context (A63).

11. In his book *Race and the Enlightenment* (1997), Emmanuel Eze contends that contemporary Kantian scholarship conveniently disregards any discussion of the racist undertones of Kant's precritical and anthropological essays. Taking his cue from David Hume, Kant notes in the section on "National Characteristics" that "[t]he Negroes of Africa have by nature no feeling that rises above the trifling" (Emmanuel Eze, ed., *Race and the Enlightenment: A Reader* [Malden, Mass.: Blackwell, 1997], 55). For a more extensive discussion of Kant's racist epistemology and aesthetics, cf. Emmanuel Eze (*Achieving Our Humanity*, 2001).

12. A derogatory, belittling word for *Frau*, woman; it is a composite of "woman" and "room."

13. In the context of colonial justifications, this has more ominous consequences: While Kant deplores slavery in his posthumously published lectures on physical geography, the Europeans as a whole are lauded for their work ethic and overall, the (male) European "has a more beautiful body, works harder, is more jocular, more controlled in his passions, more intelligent than any other race of people in the world." Eze notes correctly that Kant's racist sentiment remains the same as that displayed in the precritical *Observations* (see Eze 1997, 58).

14. Ingeborg Heidemann, *Der Begriff des Spiels und das ästhetische Weltbild in der Philosophie der Gegenwart* (Berlin, 1968), 213.

15. Although this is not a term which Kant uses in this context, I find it is useful insofar as it it appeals to the "mere" speculative, phantasmatic realm and thus cannot be applied in "dry" rigorous deductions. Kant speaks about this potential mis-use in the following: "The proud pretensions of reason, when it strives to extend its domain beyond all limits of experience, we have represented only in dry formulas that contain merely the ground of their legal claims" (A462/B490-A463/B491).

16. Trebels, 1967, 151.

17. Translator Kemp-Smith correctly points out that Kant "here plays on the double meaning of *Sinnleeres*, 'empty of sense' and 'nonsense'" (CPR, 436, n.1).

18. This critique seems to be directed against the empiricists, in particular against Hume's emotive theory.

19. Heidemann, 1968, 127.

20. Alternatively, it depicts the arbitrary, random play of ideas (cf. the section on the *Widerstreit* of cosmological ideas in CPR).

21. For the most part, I will follow Meredith's translation (1952). However, I will use the pagination of KdU.

22. Cf. Hans-Georg Gadamer, *Wahrheit und Methode*, Vol. 1 of *Gesammelte Werke* (Tübingen, 1986a, hereafter WuM).

23. Cf. also the criticisms of J. H.von Kirchmann, *Erläuterungen zu Kant's Kritik der Urtheilskraft* (Leipzig, 1882) and R. Schmidt, "Kants Lehre von der Einbildungskraft mit besonderer Rücksicht auf die Kritik der Urteilskraft" (*Annalen der Philosophie und philosophischen Kritik* 4 (1924): 1-14.

24. The possibility of communicating judgments of taste is in marked contrast to the first Critique where no references to other selves are made (cf. Wolff, *Kant's Theory of Mental Activity*).

25. Cf. Aristotle on the importance of relaxation in the *Nicomachean Ethics* (see below, Chapter 3).

26. Rudolf Makkreel, *Imagination and Interpretation in Kant: The Hermeneutical*

Import of the Critique of Judgment (Chicago: University of Chicago, 1990), 9.

27. As Crawford notes correctly, it is unclear how imagination is supposed to execute this double mental activity (Donald Crawford, *Kant's Aesthetic Theory* [Madison: University of Wisconsin, 1974], 88. Cf. also Wolff, 1963).

28. Henrich, *Aesthetic Judgment and the Moral Image of the World* (Stanford: Stanford University, 1992), 35-38.

29. Trebels, 1967, 8.

30. Makkreel, 1990, 47.

31. Cf. Gadamer, WuM, 1986a, 52.

32. I am grateful to John Brentlinger for clarifying this position.

33. Nevertheless I claim that Kant's granting imagination a certain liberty under self-chosen constraints is nothing like the Bacchanalian force Hegel reckons with in embarking in the journey of consciousness in *The Phenomenology of Spirit* or the playful, cunning free spirits that Nietzsche toys with.

34. Jest and laughter at dinner tables contribute to a speedy rumination of the food and are as such enlivening, "sensory effects on the body" (cf. Makkreel 1990, 98).

35. Makkreel, 1990, 62.

36. Makkreel, 1990, 47.

37. Makkreel, 1990, 48.

38. Unless otherwise noted, I will rely on Meredith's translation of *The Critique of Judgment* (1973).

39. Henrich, 1992, 50.

40. Jane Kneller, "Kant's Immature Imagination" in *Modern Engendering*, ed. Bat-Ami Bar On (Albany: SUNY, 1994), 149.

41. Henrich, 1992, 56.

42 . Cf. Trebel's argument, 1967, 133 and passim.

43. *Beispiele* (literally "by-plays") function prominently in Hegel, especially as "beiherspielen" (=playing alongside with, which points to unpredictable and cunning situations).

44. Trebels, 1967, 210.

45. In anticipation of Hegel's discussion of the Apollonian and Dionysian aesthetic concepts, one might want to assign Apollo to the "play of figures" or sculptures (Space), and Dionysus to the "play of sensations" (Time). This could clear up the mystery why Kant relegates music to an inferior ontological status. Thanks to Andrew Cutrofello for suggesting this point.

46. Deleuze, *Difference and Repetition* (New York: Columbia University, 1994), 145. I am grateful to Andrew Cutrofello for pointing me to Deleuze's discussion of the role of the sublime.

47 Heidegger, *Being and Time*, section 32, 150-51. Cf. also my paper, "Thrownness, Playing-in-the-world and the Question of Authenticity" in *Feminist Interpretations of Heidegger*, ed. P. Huntington and N. Holland (University Park, Pa: Penn State, 2001).

48. Deleuze, *Difference and Repetition*, 1994, 146.

49. Nietzsche does not understand the *impact* of the idea of the *principium*. Such individuating is more than a simple assigning of names to particular thoughts or rules of thought. The task of interpreting is to force a manifold into a singular "thing" which then becomes meaningful *for us*. Hence, it is not an arbitrary, innocent denotation process, but it has ideological significance. Violence thus lurks behind the rational discourse which feigns nonviolence in its disguises of orderliness and clarity. So the dichotomy of the Dionysian and Apollonian does not consist in violence and nonviolence, rather—in

Freudian terms—in manifest and latent violent expressions of play. What then is manifest violence in Kant? The feeling of the sublime? No, unlike in his pre-critical essay on the beautiful and sublime, Kant notes in the KdU that this feeling of the sublime does not arise in us when we watch the overwhelming, hideous [*gräßlich!*] waves of the ocean (KdU §23). The sublime is not contained in any sensible representations; it simply has to do with (abstract) ideas of Reason.

50. No doubt, Kant's disdain for music has autobiographical reasons: once he had to move to a new apartment, because he could not stand listening to the spiritual intonations of prisoners chanting near his home.

51. Gadamer, WuM, 1986a, 55.

52. To use a term by Zizek here, isn't it a case of fetishistic disavowal?

53. As Cutrofello notes, Kant was obsessed with disciplining bodies; he frequently bragged about his excellent physical condition: "Is it possible to conceive a human being with more perfect health than myself?" (quoted in Cutrofello, *Discipline and Critique*, 1994), 56.

54. Note the similarities of this description of play and Aristotle's approval of cathartic (tragic) play and of play as a relaxing pastime so that the player is fit for toil.

55. Cf. Winfried Sdun, "Zum Begriff des Spiels bei Kant und Schiller," *Kantstudien* 57 (1966), 500-518 and R. Seerveld "Early Kant and a Rococo Spirit: Setting for the Critique of Judgment," *Philosophical Reform* 43 (1978), 145-67.

56. Cf. Gregor's introduction to Kant, *Anthropology from a Pragmatic Point of View* (The Hague: Martinus Nijhoff, 1974), xviii-xx.

57. Sdun, 1966, 509-513.

58. Cf. Gadamer, WuM, 1986a, 88.

59. Sdun, 1966, 501. Gadamer notes that Schiller borrows the term "drive" from Fichte's doctrine of drives or impulses [*Trieblehre*] WuM, 1986a, 88.

60. "der Mensch spielt nur, wo er in voller Bedeutung des Worts Mensch ist, und er ist nur da ganz Mensch, wo er spielt."

61. Cf. Rainer Marten's important analysis of the ideological dimension of the term "menschlicher Mensch," *Der menschliche Mensch: Abschied vom utopischen Denken* (Paderborn: Schöningh, 1988), passim.

62. Cf. Helmuth Plessner, "Der Mensch im Spiel," *Das Spiel. Wirklichkeit und Methode*, ed. Werner Marx, *Freiburger Dies Universitatis*, Bd. 13, 1967, 7-11) who states that Schiller depends on the Kantian distinction of moral and natural law and on the possibility of reconciliation of classical form.

63. As I suggested below, this separation of aesthetics and ethics already occurs in Kant's work.

64. Gadamer, WuM, 1986a, 87, cf. 15th letter.

65. "So giebt uns die Natur schon in ihrem materiellen Reich ein Vorspiel des Unbegrenzten, und hebt hier schon *zum Theil* die Fesseln auf, deren sie sich im Reich der Form ganz und gar entledigt. Von dem Zwang des Bedürfnisses oder dem *physischen Ernste* nimmt sie durch den Zwang des Ueberflusses oder das *physische Spiel* den Uebergang zum ästhetischen Spiele."

66. A term I borrow from Julia Kristeva, *Powers of Horror. An Essay on Abjection* (New York: Columbia University, 1982).

67. "Das eigentliche Menschsein erfüllt sich für Schiller im Spiel, hier stellt sich die Einheit des Menschens wieder her, die Einheit von Sinnlichkeit und Vernunft, von Neigung und Pflicht, von Materialem und Formalem, von Stofftrieb und Formtrieb" (Trebels, 1967, 10).

68. Trebels, 1967, 128. Cf. my discussion of Hegel's unity of opposites in Chapter 5; Schiller's theory of drives also foreshadows Nietzsche's Apollonian and Dionysian principles.

69. Cf. Gadamer, WuM, 1986a, 88.

70. WuM, 1986a, 88.

Chapter 5

PLAY AND CUNNING IN HEGEL'S *PHENOMENOLOGY OF SPIRIT*

[Christopher Robin Milne] also resented the confusing of his childhood with popular legend: he could not remember whether it was the real or fictional Christopher Robin who invented the game of "pooh-sticks," dropping sticks from a wooden bridge into a flowing stream.
—*The Boston Globe*, April 22, 1996

As with desire,[1] philosophers have been repulsed by playful activities and attitudes at the same time that they are fascinated by them. However, Hegel not only addresses the former concept but also introduces the latter as a "serious" task. Hegel breaks with the Aristotelian malediction of play and thus sets a new ludic agenda for future artist metaphysicians (e.g., Nietzsche, Deleuze, Gadamer).

I will argue in this chapter that play is central to defining Hegel's dialectic. In fact, without understanding the centrality of play in Hegel, one cannot really grasp his concept of dialectic or of truth. Hegel, as the artist metaphysician, paves the way for the transvaluation of all values, as shown throughout the *Phenomenology of Spirit* in general and as marked by the playfulness of the artwork sections in particular. Following Eugen Fink's phenomenological insight, I maintain that Hegel's concepts are constantly "on the move," making it impossible to force anything into tight, steady definitions. Such "conceptual failure" is exemplified in truth's cunning mask as a Bacchanalian revel, whose ambiguous meaning with respect to the dialectical process has puzzled generations of Hegel scholars.

The abundance of play metaphors in the *Phenomenology of Spirit* (hereafter, PhS) has been ignored by most Hegel scholars. Notable exceptions are phenomenologists such as Heidegger (1970), who concentrate on the terms of play of forces (*Spiel der Kräfte*), example, or instance (*Beispiel*) and Hegel's own creation of the term *beiherspielen* (playing along, by-play). In various lectures on the PhS, Eugen Fink (1977a and 1977b) has also given some attention to this notion. In recent years, though, Hegel's laughter (Flay), Hegel's myopic traveler (Butler), his mockery (Desmond), his manipulator (Zizek), his mask as

Nietzschean Satyagraha (Cutrofello) have surfaced, creating space for a fresh reading of the *Phenomenology*. With the help of these playful "experiments," much of Hegel's work has unleashed multiple voices; they see themselves as undoing the deconstructivist indictment (especially by Derrida 1982) that Hegel's program represents as the epitomy of logocentrism. Desmond (1992) convincingly argues that Hegel's mockery of philosophy, of Kantian and Platonic philosophy in particular, foreshadows Nietzsche's indictment of Platonism in his *Birth of Tragedy*. Deleuze (1983), on the other hand, narrowly views Hegel's dialectic as carrying a notion of *ressentiment* and a "spirit of gravity," thus being antithetical to Nietzsche's project. My reading differs from these Hegelian studies insofar as I focus on play and use this concept to challenge the conception of the dialectical movement as carrying the spirit of gravity. I argue that Hegel's dialectic is greatly influenced by Heraclitus and inspired by Euripidian imagery; by tarrying with the negative, Hegel plays with the ephemeral, the fleeting moment that might disguise itself in the mask of the spirit of gravity but it does not necessarily have to be confined to this mask.[2]

In the preface of the *Phenomenology*, Hegel proclaims his goal to make philosophizing a serious business again (§67). Supposedly, this means, as he says elsewhere, that philosophy is not an "empty game" or a "restless activity of empty reflection" (Hegel 1965, 5), merely engaged in superficial diatribes. Yet, the True is "the Bacchanalian revel" (§47)—and philosophers, engaged in this frenzy, take this game seriously. In order to assume this mask, though, it is necessary to overcome opinions, via determinate negation, such as the following one, mocked by Hegel: "We do not esteem playfulness as something sublime but as something of lower standing over and against the form of thought."[3]

Hegel tries to qualify what he considers a good, authentic playful act and toys with notions of seriousness and mere superficial play or leisure. For instance, the life of the absolute and divine knowledge or cognition are equivalents of "a play of love with itself"; yet this idea sinks to the mere "edification" or even "trifle," if this image fails to emphasize the seriousness, pain, work involved in negating the negation (§19). There is also another important aspect to this phenomenological game. Notably, Hegel performs, just like Tony Curtis and Jack Lemmon in Billy Wilder's *Some Like It Hot*, in such a way that he never repeats his cunning past the point of revealing his trick, since "repetition of a conjuring trick already seen through is intolerable" (cf. §51).

Hegelian scholarship of the PhS has intermittently engaged with the notion of play but has not looked through the lense of play, as it were, except for a sustained effort by Eugen Fink. The notion of truth being disguised in the form of play (*Spiel*) has been taken up by Martin Heidegger in his analysis of the difficult section "Force and Understanding" of the PhS. He interprets the meaning of the term "play of forces" as "the true, the actual [which] is the play [of forces], the center which keeps together the extremes in relation to each other."[4] Eugen Fink goes even further, insofar as he does not rest his ludic case with consciousness's move toward self-consciousness via a process called *Spiel der Kräfte*, but asserts that Hegel strategically employs the notions of circle and play within the realm of Reason (*Vernunft*) in order to characterize Reason as play. In the later parts of the PhS Hegel's metaphor of play is foundational for under-standing of the self-moving Concept *(Begriff)*. The activity of self-reflective self-consciousness or Reason is, as Hegel puts it, a playful circular motion: "Action has . . . the appearance of the movement of a circle which moves freely within itself in a void, which, unimpeded, now expands, now contracts, and is perfectly content to [play] in and with its own self" (PhS, §396). So, the move-ment of Reason, Fink concludes, "which appears as a movement of work, strug-gle, love and overcoming of death, is determined in its total character as play."[5] This kind of game Hegel plays, Fink states, is Dionysian and Heraclitean.

I argue that both Fink and Heidegger miss noting the deployment of playful-ness as a cunning, mocking, elusive trope which masks the true—i.e., they do not comment on the humorous, comic character of Hegel's play. Clearly, play figures prominently in Hegel's *Bildungsroman*;[6] he dares to include playfulness in his dialectical method—invoking a movement that plays-along-with[7] *and* transgresses the boundaries of Aristotelian metaphysics.[8] I argue that his usage of play and seriousness as mockery of philosophy foreshadows the tactics of the artist-metaphysicians (Nietzsche, Fink, Gadamer) to intertwine, rather than use to contrast, the opposites play-seriousness. In Nietzsche's work we see that Hegel's Bacchanalian revel reappears as a Dionysian, life-affirming dance (cf. *Birth*) and that Truth masks itself as a woman (cf. *Genealogy of Morals*).

To understand Hegel's mockery of Truth—in particular of the correspon-dence theory of truth[9]—in his quest of the Absolute is to realize that the *Phe-nomenology* narrates a series of deceptions, fiction, and false belief, and ulti-mately of failure.[10] Hegel engages in a game without victors, without closure; instead he stresses the playful movement of consciousness, full of discontinui-ties, ruptures, changes (§§184-88). Hegel's play with a systematic approach of science, with totality ("das Wahre ist das Ganze"), with absolute knowledge—which irritates and infuriates Deconstructionists—is but one other disguise, masking of his narrative(s). In fact, in his comedy, farcical play, also known as "The Phenomenology of Spirit," Hegel masters par excellence the art of cunning and catches his opponents off guard—with lime-twigs (cf. §73).

The coupling of play and seriousness is most prominently displayed in his discussion of the aesthetic dimension of religion, in particular in the section en-titled "Kunstreligion" (in the seventh chapter on Religion). In the section "The Spiritual Work of Art," Hegel dwells on the representation of necessity qua unity of the concept by using the image of the "play of its actions [sc. of indi-vidual moments] which retains its earnestness and worth" (§732). Elsewhere, he says of the cultus: "The cultus [is] a serious playing and a playful seriousness, a gravity that is gay" (*Philosophy of Religion*, Vol. I, 168).

In my commentary of the relevant sections on the sacred character of play, (cf. section on the spiritual artwork §§727-47) I will take up Desmond's book *Beyond Hegel and Dialectic* (1992) which talks about a related topic: the comic and the religious mask(s) of philosophy. Desmond emphasizes the radical ten-sion between religion and philosophy, where both (faith contra reason) "mirror each other in a positive manner which shows them to dialectically converge in the middle."[11] This convergence means that they both come to share the identity of the other, i.e., philosophy cannot dismiss faith (speculative thought), and religion cannot do without thought of the absolute even if that means to risk losing faith.[12] Rather than heeding Desmond's call of "think[ing] beyond the masks and the slanders,"[13] we should *seriously* play with the masks Hegel provides us—another expression of "tarrying with the negative."

Hegel is the first speculative thinker (in the Western philosophical tradition) to break with the Aristotelian malediction of play. Recognizing this requires a rereading of Hegel's absolute idealism and systematicity and a more literal interpretation of the "cunning of the Idea" (*List der Idee*) than is usually presented. Hegel's play theory has a proto-Nietzschean character; in fact, Hegel's play serves as a nodal point by breaking with Kantian subjectivism and creating the conditions of possibility of diverging play discourses, e.g., of a play of the self and a play of the world. It is not just a one-sided subjectivist play (of the genius) à la Kant, but a play where the self sees itself realized in the Absolute, externalizes itself in substantial, objective nature.[14]

First, I will provide an analysis of the trope of the Bacchanalian revel and explore the relevance of Heraclitus's dialectics and Euripides' play *The Bacchae* for Hegel. Secondly, I use as a historical *Beispiel* Hegel's interpretation of the Hellenic era's so-called art-religion (*Kunstreligion*) in the form of epos, tragedy, and comedy. The final section of this chapter is devoted to an ideology critique of Hegel's play, e.g., with respect to his romanticization of the Greeks—that only they knew how to genuinely play.[15]

The Bacchanalian Revel

In the Preface of the PhS, Hegel introduces the famous metaphor of the Bacchanalian revel, which seems to underscore his similarity to Nietzsche. The question is whether this revel is only formulaic, an extravagant expression or whether in fact it explores Dionysian frenzy and gives important clues about Hegel's conceptualization of dialectics. I will quote the paragraph which mentions the trope almost in its entirety:

> [The philosophical movement] is the process which begets and traverses its own moments, and this whole movement constitutes what is positive [in it] and its truth. This truth therefore includes the negative also, what would be called the false, if it could be regarded as something from which one might abstract. The evanescent itself must, on the contrary, be regarded as essential, not as something fixed, cut off from the True, and left lying who knows where outside it, any more than the True is to be regarded as something on the other side, positive and dead. Appearance is the arising and passing away that does not itself arise and pass away, but is "in itself" [i.e., subsists intrinsically], and constitutes the actuality and the movement of the life of truth. *The True is thus the Bacchanalian revel in which no member is not drunk; yet because each member collapses as soon as [it] drops out, the revel is just as much transparent and simple repose* [emphasis added]. [*Das Wahre ist so der bacchantische Taumel, an dem kein Glied nicht trunken ist; und weil jedes, indem es sich absondert, ebenso unmittelbar [sich]*

auflöst, ist er ebenso die durchsichtige und einfache Ruhe.] (PhS §47, trans. Miller)

As Richard Norman (1976) points out, this passage is central in defining dialectics, even though Hegel does not mention the term specifically at this point in the preface of PhS. The dialectical movement "is the dynamic aspect of the 'system' and its 'necessity.'" Oddly, the revel (*der Taumel*) "is just as much a state of transparent unbroken calm."[16] What Norman fails to look at is how this dynamism is employed here: what is noteworthy is actually Hegel's allusion to a dialectical interplay of chance and necessity, reminding us of the Nietzschean interpellation of the "iron dice of necessity." The revel which defines the true, displays the peculiar Hegelian brand of dialectics, since it is not only the frantic movement from one form of consciousness to the other but also constitutes an aspect of stasis and systematicity. William Desmond (1992), too, recognizes the importance of revel in the PhS, and points to the Bacchanalian revel as a dialectical metaphor since it states a *coincidentia oppositorum*.[17] Desmond notes that this metaphor "also points us to what is Other to dialectical logic in that its enigmatic, ambiguous power springs from a *persisting doubleness* that resists reduction to univocity, even a 'higher' mediated univocity. This religious metaphor images the cult of philosophy as beyond logicist impiousness and as turned towards what is Other to philosophy."[18] This Otherness is the performative enactment of what Desmond calls "the agapeic excess of the original power of being."[19] The agapeic absolute (as opposed to the erotic absolute[20]) is "the affirmative indeterminacy of inexhaustibility, i.e., overdetermination . . . of plenitude in itself."[21]

Desmond also notes that Hegel's dialectic bears a philosophical mask which is the mask of the comic. Dialectic, he states, "articulates the logos of failure and the failure of logos."[22] This is a poignant assessment of the dialectical movement displayed in the metaphor of Bacchanalian revel. Tarrying with the negative moment of the dialectic, the self is immersed in this *Taumel*—tumbling because all foundations are shaken, she fails to be in control of her own movements—a limit experience which is both divine and terrifying at the same time. This is the cunning journey that Bacchus toys with: At every stage throughout the Phenomenology, self-consciousness realizes that its point of departure at every turn is always already a failure. Since we have touched upon shaken (epistemological) foundations, let us now turn to the thinker who introduced the doctrine of flux.

Heraclitus's Unity of Opposites and the Interplay of Dionysus and Apollo

In order to understand Hegel's *Auseinandersetzung* (engagement) with play in the PhS, it is pertinent to take into account his "peculiar adoption of Heraclitus."[23] Although Heraclitus is not explicitly mentioned in the PhS, he is, I argue, nevertheless "omnipresent." Perhaps, though, Hegel takes a cue from a Heraclitean fragment which comments on the foolish practice of the Bacchic revels:

> If it were not in honor of Dionysus that they conducted the procession, and sang the phallic hymn, their activity would be completely shameless. But Hades is Dionysus, in whose honor they rave and perform the Bacchic revels. (B15)

Hegel did in fact hold Heraclitus in high esteem; in the *Lectures on the History of Philosophy* (hereafter HP), he states emphatically: "Here we see land; there is no proposition of Heraclitus that I have not adopted in my Logic" (HP, 279). Hegel claims that Heraclitus grasps "the Absolute itself as just this process of the dialectic itself" (HP, 278). The dialectical process is important to this Presocratic thinker, because, unlike the Eleatics, he focuses on the notion of Becoming (and Evanescence), from which he derives his theory of the flux and the unity of opposites. Hegel declares that Zeno's dialectic is still only immanent and subjective, whereas Heraclitus's dialectic is objective, using a process of attaining truth by refuting previously held viewpoints. Hegel argues that Heraclitus's speculative thought is not limited to a philosophy of nature, "where the simple substance in fire and the other elements in itself becomes metamorphosed" (HP, 290); his philosophy is the first to articulate "the unity of the principle of consciousness and of the object" (HP, 293). Hegel describes it approvingly as a "beautiful, natural, child-like manner of speaking truth of the truth" (HP, 293).

Howard Williams (1989) argues that Hegel adopted the doctrine of flux and the unity of opposites from this Presocratic philosopher, as evinced by such works as *The Philosophy of Right* and *The Science of Logic*. I will make use of Williams' analysis by applying it to the PhS and in particular to our passage in question.

In the passage of the revel (§47), Hegel describes dialectics as a constantly changing cyclical movement, as "the process which begets and traverses its own moments, and this whole movement constitutes what is positive [in it] and its truth." What is a positive shape might come into being through its very negation. Hegel illustrates this point with his play of the fleeting, vanishing moment: "The evanescent itself must . . . be regarded as essential, not as something fixed, cut off from the True, and left lying who knows where outside it, any more than the True is to be regarded as something on the other side, positive and dead. Appearance is the arising and passing away . . . ." Clearly, his dialectic is characterized by the necessity of appearances and by the proposition that all that is contradictory is real. Similarly, Heraclitus states that "everything is moving and nothing stays still, and that one cannot step twice into the same river" (B91). Both thinkers espouse a dialectic riddled with a play of differences, in particular toying with dialectical metaphors in form of a coincidence of opposites. Note for instance the ambivalent character of the "simple certainty" of Spirit in the Classical Greek period: it is defined as a "serene existence [*ruhiges Bestehen*] and as absolute unrest [*absolute Unruhe*] . . ." (PhS §701).

Since change and movement play such an important part in the Hegelian phenomenological perspective of consciousness and reality, rigid definitions could never provide what Williams calls "a continually critical and open-ended approach."[24] He argues that Heraclitus's doctrine of flux cannot be separated arbitrarily from the apparent paradoxical idea of the unity of opposites,[25] and Hegel too thinks them together. As the above quote on the evanescent (*das Verschwindende*) makes clear, the dialectical movement is determined as much by its positive moments as by its negative ones; there are several fragments that support the claim of the importance of this doctrine for Heraclitus (e.g., "The purest and foulest water: for fish drinkable and life-sustaining; for men undrinkable and deadly."). Heraclitus's "tarrying with the negative"—by not only juxtaposing life-affirming and life-threatening elements ("Hades is Dionysus"—death is life), but by reflecting on the positive value of the negative—makes him so congenial to Hegel who says in his *Logic* (hereafter SL) that the dialectical nature of reason is such that it subverts the "determinations of the understanding"; nevertheless reason does not remain "in the nothingness of this result but in the result is no less positive." (SL, 28). Hegel explicitly refers to dialectics as the unity of opposites (SL, 56).

The cunning appeal to the proposition of the unity of opposites not only characterizes Heraclitean dialectics but also the Hegelian "movement of the life of truth," i.e., the Bacchanalian revel which is frenzied movement and controlled repose at the same time. No other passage characterizes this unity of opposites better than the discussion of the "simple substance of life" (PhS §171), which Fink rightly links to the revel. Hegel states that "[t]hus the simple substance of Life is the splitting-up of itself into shapes and at the same time the dissolution of these existent differences; and the dissolution of the splitting-up is just as much a splitting-up and a forming of members." In this passage, Hegel alludes to the positive meaning of the notion of diremption: "the supersession of individual existence is equally the production of it." Or, the process of life is "just as much an imparting of shape [*Gestaltung*] as a supersession of it." New shapes are developed out of the vanishing of the primary shape. ["Entzweiung . . . *und zugleich* Auflösung . . ." §171, emphasis added.] In Hegelian jargon, this organological thinking amounts to the formula of birth (thesis) plus death (antithesis) equals life (synthesis).[26]

Hyppolite, too, attributes special significance to the unity of opposites in the revel metaphor. He points out the agonistic character of the relationship of the opposites, faith, and intellection (that is the struggle between *Aufklärung*, Enlightenment, and *Aberglaube*, superstition) exemplified in the study of the self-alienated Spirit (in the section on Culture and Alienation).

The supreme synthesis of Hegel's thought is this unity of *movement* and *repose*, a unity of the disquiet of the self (temporality) and the eternity of essence. For this reason truth in-and-for-itself is "Bacchic delirium . . . but this delirium is also a translucent and simple repose." . . . The two moments separate here as essence and self, faith and intellection.[27]

In his secular interpretation of the PhS, Eugen Fink puts much weight into a cosmological, Heraclitean reading of the image of the Bacchanalian revel. It is "the life-absorbing [*lebenstrunken*, i.e., literally, "life-drunken"] movement of Being, which traverses all things; it is the incessant movement, which pushes all Being-in-itself away into Being-for-itself, and is at the same time the 'simple repose', as which the Being-in-itself lets occur all changes in themselves and conserves itself in all of them, at the same time undermining them."[28] Fink carefully avoids an anthropocentric reading of *Glied* and advances this view in his book *Sein und Mensch* (1977b), where he integrates Heraclitean and Nietzschean imagery in this passage: "The True is the Bacchanalian revel, i.e., the Dionysian movement of Being, which floods all entities; the revel creates and destroys it, and it is at the same time 'simple repose.'"[29] Fink argues that this playful metaphor is used by Hegel to elucidate his speculative concept of world or cosmos.[30]

But the revel not only falls into the dimension of world, Being, and truth; it also determines Life as such. Fink points to the expression of "allgemeine Leben" (universal life; cf. PhS §171) or, in Fink's words, "All-Leben" (totality of life) where Hegel discusses the process of life as involving diremption into various shapes and as the dissolution of the shapes' existing differences. Here, the revel appears as life, as a circular life-process of creation and destruction. Hence, Fink concludes that Hegel repeats an existential, fundamental experience of Heraclitus.[31]

Although Fink provides us with a rich and original reading of Hegelian dialectics, I miss a discussion of the struggle of oppositional forces which pertains to the metaphor of the Bacchanalian frenzy. It is not clear whether the Dionysian is struggling with something other than itself. Fink is ambiguous about the meaning of the revel's relationship with the Dionysian and does not explain what is Dionysian about "simple repose." In other words, Fink does not seem to think that the Apollonian aspect has any significance for Hegel.

In the Preface, we are told that the true is the whole; Hegel clearly mocks the traditional correspondence theory of truth.[32] A few pages later, we hear that the true is defined as a revel of a special sort, and if we restrict our interpretation to Hegel's aesthetics, these descriptions suddenly make sense. The interplay of contingency and necessity or of drunken frenzy and calm repose, I mentioned earlier, turns out to depict the life forces of Dionysus and Apollo, to borrow Nietzschean concepts here. In *The Birth of Tragedy*, Nietzsche explains that Apollo's *principium individuationis* applies to the transparency and simple repose of the revel, providing the order, harmony and shape, whereas Dionysus's principle is that of chaos, drunkenness, frenzy, or simply uncontrolled motion. In the PhS, these opposing life forces are portrayed as negative (Dionysian) and positive (Apollonian) moments. Hegel emphasizes that negativity carries the notion of becoming (*Enstehung*) and positivity is attributed to what is factically dead, the state of calm repose. (For further elaboration of this point, see below in the section on "art religion.") The unity of movement and repose is a key marker to this dialectical play; in fact, as Hyppolite observes, it represents "[t]he supreme synthesis of Hegel's thought."[33] Yet, these moments should not be thought of as being in a binary opposition as they are depicted in Nietzsche's *Birth*; with his emphasis on "tarrying with the negative," Hegel is much closer to the Heraclitean logic of flow and destruction.[34] This point will be clarified in the section on the abstract artwork (below).

The revel thus depicts the Concept *(Begriff)* or absolute Notion, which else-where is characterized as the simple essence of life that "pulsates within itself but does not move, inwardly trembles, yet is at rest" (§162). Hence the Concept not only reconciles the opposites (of Apollo and Dionysus) but also is *the* differ-ence ("das vielmehr selbst alle Unterschiede ist"). Clearly, *both* aesthetic princi-ples determine "the whole of the movement," which is the "movement of the life of truth" or alternatively, the self-realization of the spirit. In fact, the cunning of the Idea or Reason (cf. below) is actualized insofar as Reason uses both princi-ples as playthings to capriciously arrange a unity of these opposites. I argue then that Hegel lays the groundwork for "deviant" philosophical engagement with play—and I am thinking of play as characterized by the so-called artist meta-physicians Nietzsche, Fink, and Gadamer—and even if Hegel may not totally break with the logocentric, paidio-phobic tradition, he at least deviates from its Apollonian path playfully.

The Cunning of Reason and Euripides's "God of Many Names"

In this section I will look at anthropocentric readings of the Bacchanalian revel. I will use Zizek's psychoanalytic reading of the "cunning of reason" and apply it to my analysis of Hegel's employment of Dionysus, by studying the characteris-tics of this god in Euripides' play *The Bacchae*. First, I will again focus on the Bacchanalian revel. This image jumps up out of nowhere in §47, and quite strikingly, Hegel employs this metaphor to describe "the True" *(das Wahre)*. What is this member and its relationship to the whirl? In his translation of the sentence, A.V. Miller provides an anthropocentric interpretation of the term "member" *(das Glied)*, by rendering the German "und weil jedes, indem es sich absondert, ebenso unmittelbar [sich] auflöst" into "yet because each member collapses as soon as he drops out" (§47). Miller suggests that this whirl envelops each Bacchic dancer with such destructive force that he has to give up dancing and collapses due to physical exhaustion. Although the member partaking in the revel could be an active human player, it is plausible that humans appear as pas-sive playthings that are being toyed with. They appear to be delivered over to the whim of the revel, which imposes a Bacchantic force over everything—not merely humans—within its reach. The revel assumes then the position of a cos-mic play akin to Heraclitus's *aion* where the players are not relevant, but the play as such is. So play qua revel is subject—not the player qua *Glied* config-ured in a concatenation. In other words, it is a cosmic game where players in-evitably drop out in the course of the game and become irrelevant. This game recapitulates the course of the PhS, which narrates how the various shapes of consciousness lose their relevance, once the Concept (qua finite reason) takes hold.[35] Zizek provides a nuanced reading of the relationship of those human members being toyed with by the revel or the Absolute. With respect to Hegel's famous allusion to the dialectical interplay of subject and substance, e.g., "everything turns on grasping and expressing the True, not only as *Substance*, but equally as *Subject*" (PhS, §17), Zizek asserts that

> [t]his does not mean that the Absolute itself is a Subject playing with us, finite humans, i.e., that, in the movement of absolute reflection, we, finite humans, make ourselves into the instrument, the medium through which the Absolute contemplates itself—this would be a simple perverse position. What Hegel has in mind is that the split between us and the Absolute (the split on account of which we are subjects) is at the same time the self-split of the Absolute itself: *we participate at the Absolute not on account of our exalted contemplation of it, but by means of the very gap which forever separates us from it*—as in Kafka's novels where the fascinated gaze of the subject is already included in the functioning of the transcendent, unapproachable agency of Law (the court, the castle).[36]

The Hegelian subject's relationship to the Substance is such that it provides a reification of the Substance, an externalization. To understand the role-playing one assumes "in the game of the 'cunning of reason',"[37] Zizek looks at Hegel's notion of the *act* which involves jumping into the unknown and the externalizing of the self, insofar as it plays alongside other selves, communicates with them in order to find out one's own desires, values, since—as learnt from Freud—one does not have some privileged access to the truth about oneself.

Hegel elaborates the term "cunning of reason" in *The Philosophy of History* in his analysis of historical struggles between concrete selves. Individuals may think they follow their own rational plans that they enact; instead they are duped into following and legitimating the master plan of the idea, the divine plan. In economic terms, this means that an artisan believes that he produces to accumulate wealth and takes steps to achieve this goal (by exploiting nature and perhaps his apprentices), but in fact he takes part unwittingly in the development of productive societal forces, i.e., the "objectivization of spirit." This is a clue to the seductive appeal of Hegel's play: laying out the functioning of the dialectics of truth and deception. As Zizek explains, "the deception is just a game Idea plays with itself. Idea realizes its true ends by means of the 'cunning of reason.'"[38] But ultimately, the dialectical game is a failure: there is no being who is the supreme manipulator, i.e., who is beyond deception. Zizek emphatically declares that "the manipulator [even God] himself is always-already manipulated."[39] Hence, it is a mistake to assume that there is a grand puppeteer (the Absolute) who is not subjected to the subject-substance oppositional relationship and simply toys with the human playthings. Everybody, even the dialectician, is an integral member of the game that produces truth through deception.

Zizek's sophisticated reading of the "cunning of reason" should prove useful for an interpretation of Hegel's use of Dionysian imagery. The Dionysian revel casts a magic spell and masks the rules to show that the terror of the negative does indeed contain nothing positive. Hegel, who refers to Bacchanalian revelry repeatedly throughout the PhS, must have had in mind a passage from Euripides' *The Bacchae*, where Teiresias praises the divine prophesies of Dionysus, which enrapture those mortals who take part in the Bacchanalian mysteries:

> And this god is a prophet, too: the *Bacchic*
> *frenzy* gives the power of foresight; when
> Bacchus fully infiltrates the body
> of whoever is possessed, they foretell the future.
> (lines 298ff., C.K. Williams trans., emphasis added)

Bacchus, the trickster—not Apollo—determines the outcome, accomplished in a transparent manner in order to feign harmony, not chaos. The individual member of this game or dance lacks subjectivity, is not *für sich*. The player does not control the game, rather dissipates, dissolves; he has a fleeting presence. In this way, Dionysus uses Pentheus as his tool; however, Pentheus taunts the god and grants him access, lets himself be invaded by this alien, parasitical life force.

This image of the dissolving movement appears frequently in the latter part of the PhS (notably in chapter 6, "Spirit: Self-alienated Spirit"); Hegel brings up the disintegration of consciousness and connects it to play, e.g., *das sich auflösende Spiel* (poorly translated as "nihilistic game" by Miller—even the Hegelian play with the "negation of negation" is not nihilistic). In a section on *Bildung* (culture), we find a most intriguing parallel to the revel image. True Spirit, Hegel asserts, tears apart, insofar as it forces "all of those moments, which are supposed to count as essence [*Wesen*] and actual *members* of the whole, to dissolve" (§521, my emphasis). Note that as in the revel imagery, members are again put to task to dissolve themselves; but dissipation involves taking on another shape (*Gestalt*)—this is the significance of the (positive) movement of the "negation of negation."[40]

Dionysus, again, is at play here, in the form of "torn consciousness" which speaks in a cunning and witty (*geistreich*) manner. The name of the game, Hegel alludes to (cf. §594), is, of course, the Jacobinical terror, involving a diabolical brutality—not unlike the relentless judgments which Dionysus hands down to King Pentheus of Thebes and his mother Agave (cf. the god's final speech in *The Bacchae*). This destructive (*zerreissende*) judgment is, Hegel tells us, "what amounts to the true and invincible, while it overpowers everything." Again, the true, as told in the revel image, amounts to the truth of a *mainomenos Dionusos*, a truth that is utterly destructive and inflicts madness, *mania*, and thus ultimately causes its own dissolution.

Perhaps Hegel is playing with some of the many attributes of the god, when he writes about *Zerrissenheit* and *Auflösung*. One of Dionysus's many names is *anthroporraistes* (someone who tears apart humans) and—more positively— *lusios* (someone who loosens knots, ties; who liberates).[41] What Hegel stresses here is a truly Dionysian feature, namely transgression, hinted at with terms such as "dissolving game" and "disrupted consciousness." Just as Dionysus takes possession of Pentheus's mother, who tears apart her beloved son, so does the external revolutionary terror, as a "kind of parasitical, malign foreign body,"[42] intrude the subject's consciousness. The "sheer terror of the negative" contains nothing positive, but this negation "is not something alien" to the self (PhS §594).

Thus is the significance of the negation of negation: "what first appears as an external obstacle reveals itself to be an inherent hindrance, i.e., an outside force turns into an inner compulsion."[43]

Zizek's point is perhaps best illustrated with *The Bacchae* by Euripides. In this play, Dionysus and Bacchic revelry exemplify the movement of internalization. Dionysus's personae cling on parasitically to some morally bad trait (e.g., Pentheus's sacrilegious arrogance) and make a mockery out of it; Dionysus's sadistic display of force transforms into the masochistic desire of a condemned subject. Yet, Euripides still relies on the art of make-believe and the notion that masks actually disguise or hide some real face, which is no longer the case in Hegel's post-Platonic ludic world. (I will come back to the role of masks in a later section of this chapter.)

The metaphor of the Bacchanalian revel clearly assumes a central category in the PhS, especially in light of Hegel's play theory. As I see it, this passage of the revel in the PhS foremost points to the cunning of Hegel's work. Play as the Other of reason marks its entry into philosophical discourse, forcing us to re-think the dialectical movement and its deployment in Hegel's *Bildungsroman*.

In the following section I will discuss Hegel's depiction of play in the Art-Religion chapter. This chapter all too often is overlooked mainly because Hegel is thought to have a more mature aesthetical analysis in his later works. However, where we encounter a merely fleeting presence of the Apollonian and Dionysian forces in earlier chapters, Hegel now fleshes them out in the section on Greek tragedy and comedy; furthermore he provides a sociohistorical analysis of his play with subjectivity. Westphal (1979) is correct in pointing out that we have to read the PhS as a coherent work which gives an analysis of transcendental subjectivity and states that it cannot be thought of as separate from its social history (187).

Notes on Art-Religion

Play appears most prominently in "spiritual" forms of art, i.e., epics, tragedy, and comedy, in the section on art-religion (*Kunstreligion*). *Kunstreligion* is the term Hegel uses to depict the interplay of religious and artistic expressions of consciousness in a particular historical period, namely classical Greece.[44] He subdivides the section further into the abstract work of art, the living work of art (*das lebendige Kunstwerk*), and the spiritual work of art in order to describe the development of (aesthetic) consciousness within Greek culture. Spiritual artwork (*das geistige Kunstwerk*), the third and highest form of art-religion, is relevant for our discussion because of the occurrence of the Bacchanalian frenzy in Greek tragedy. (In the previous section, I have hinted at the importance of tragedy for Hegel by introducing Euripides' play.) Yet, playful expressions surface in the preceding lower forms, i.e., in the abstract and living works of art, where Hegel obliquely presents the opposite principles of Apollonian and Dionysian art.

Kunstreligion is one of three subdivisions of chapter seven (Religion) in the PhS. The significance of the entire chapter of religion is, as Hyppolite (1974) notes, Hegel's replay—in concentrated form—of the development of the journey of consciousness, or rather of spirit.[45] Hegel distinguishes between natural religion (Eastern religions, as practiced in ancient Indian, Persian, Egyptian cultures), which he compares to the state of natural consciousness, and art-religion (Greek tragedy and comedy), which corresponds to self-consciousness, and finally revealed religion (Christianity), which corresponds to Reason. In this section I will only discuss the appearance of play in religion in the form of art. It is noteworthy, however, that in the chapter on natural religions play appears as "essence-less by-play in substance," (*ein wesenloses Beihersphielen an dieser Substanz*) which refers to the "revelling life" which is not yet for-itself, i.e., a self-conscious subject (§§687-88). Here, we find one of the rare occurrences of a malediction of *Beiherspielen*, a term that Hegel coined and which is usually reserved for a positive dynamic movement of self-consciousness. In this passage, play as "essence-less playing alongside with," is *not yet* good, agonistic performance. What it indicates, moreover, Hegel's discussion of a (moral) progression of forms of religions—from "instinctual" natural religion (manifest in ancient Indian, Persian and Egyptian cultures) to "revealed" religion (Christianity—sine Judaism!)—is a display of culturally imperialist attitudes on his part.[46] In this historical evaluation of pre-Christian religious consciousness, only Greek so-called "*Kunstreligion*" is exempted from malediction, since "the play of rites or actions [*Handlungen*] receives its earnestness and worth in the actions themselves" (§732).

What is the significance of the connection between art and religion? In his chapter "Religion: Mysticism or Humanism?," Hyppolite states that religion figures prominently as a form of art in the PhS. It is only much later that Hegel clearly differentiates between art and religion. But even then, e.g., in his various lectures on religion, he is preoccupied with the tripartite semiautonomous spheres of art, religion, and philosophy. Hegel adds art and play (tragedy, etc.) to the long chapter on religion, because religion in its "superior" form is synonymous with the work of art. Desmond explains that "Greek *Kunstreligion* is not art in the post-Kantian sense of a specialized realm of aesthetic experience. The aesthetic and the mythic, that is, the religious, cannot be separated."[47] Hegel states that religion in the form of art plays in—or rather with—the margins of rationality, where the (Egyptian) artisan-turned (Hellenic) spiritual worker has given up on blending "the heterogeneous forms of thought and natural objects" (PhS §699). Natural or instinctual religion has developed into a higher form, namely, "artificial" (*künstliche*) religion (cf. §683).

In his lectures on religion, Hegel refers to art-religion, i.e., whenever he describes Greek religion, as religion of beauty. He invokes images of a playful people whose initiation rites, the Eleusian mysteries, and other sacral festivals produce enjoyment, "immediate gratification," and conjure up fantasies of ideal beauty.[48] In his later work, Hegel does not maintain the rather rigid characterization of Greek art-religion as the abstract, living, and spiritual work of art, where the spiritual work represents the highest form of art-religion. In the introductory passages of the "*Kunstreligion*" chapter in the PhS (cf. §§699-704), Hegel emphatically dispels the naturalistic, mythical "monsters in shape, word, and deed" (§698) by invoking a new shape of consciousness, the affirmative Hellenic lifestyle, its joie de vivre; art-religion conjures up the ethical Spirit of a playful, artistic Greek polis and its artworks: "The Spirit [of Greece] is the free nation [*Volk*] in which hallowed custom constitutes the substance of all, whose actuality and existence each and everyone knows to be his own will and deed" (§700). This ethical spirit embodies a happy equilibrium of "humanity which is perfect in its finitude, but it is an unstable equilibrium, the youth of world spirit."[49] In this precious moment, Dionysian frivolity breaks out: the dissolution of all existing, firm boundaries of the ethical order; transgression of enjoyment, and display of absolute giddiness (*Leichtsinn*). Note the Heraclitean playfulness, the dialectics of the opposites (the Apollonian and Dionysian forces), in the following sentence: "This simple certainty of Spirit within itself has a twofold meaning [*das Zweideutige*]: it is a serene, stable existence and settled truth, and also absolute unrest and the passing-away [*Vergehen*] of the ethical order" (§701). This equilibrium of this play between the extremes does not last, however. The Bacchanalian skirmish as one of the extremes wins control over the ethical substance. Apollonian *principium individuationis* fails to deliver a crucial message to the self, namely, its ability to recognize itself as a free, liberated substance. Experiencing this sudden negation of enjoyment, of self-trust, Spirit mourns over the loss of its giddy Dasein (§701). The exuberant sentiment of this passage certainly echoes the romanticist "back to Ancient Greece" movement of Schleiermacher, Schiller, and Winckelmann, but Hegel notes that the very collapse of giddiness (of consciousness) into absolute unrest and melancholia is the condition of possibility of absolute art (§702).[50] As Cutrofello (1996) points out, for Hegel, unlike for Schiller, there is no return to a mythic Greece.[51]

Absolute art's first moment is manifest in the form of the *abstract work of art*. The artwork is abstract, because the artist has not yet recognized his own subjective expression in the work. He fails to see the dialectical relationship between the artistic creation and the self-conscious activity of the productive process (§§708-9). The abstract artwork appears in two extreme instantiations, namely, in that of the ephemeral hymn and in that of the objective, reified statue. Again, note the interplay of opposites, of dynamic and static aspects, in this art form. Furthermore, the statue represents pure exteriority, pure repose of a divine figur; the hymn expresses lyrically the god's pure interiority, pure feelings (§714). Hyppolite notes that "the contrast between Apollonian and Dionysian art already appears in these passages," i.e., in the discussion of the opposition between sculpture and lyricism (in the abstract work of art) and in later passages on the living work of art. It is noteworthy that the opposites of lyricism and sculpture are also, as Hyppolite points out correctly, important examples for Nietzsche's theory on Apollonian and Dionysian art in his *Birth of Tragedy*.[52] For Hegel, these opposites are unified, mediated in *Andacht* (worship) in the abstract cult (§715, §719). Another Nietzschean resemblance in the play of opposites is when Hegel describes the rite in this way: "The cultus [is] a serious playing and a playful seriousness, a gravity that is gay" (*Philosophy of Religion*, Vol. I, 168). Dionysian exuberance is inevitably linked to Apollonian ascetism.

In the performance of the sacrifice, the notion of enjoyment resurfaces again, that is, bearing the mask of a cunning, vanishing mediator[53] where even foul play seems to be involved. The rite appears to demand from the sacrificing person a total surrender of the gift to the gods. However,

> this is only a small part, and the other act of sacrifice is merely the destruction of what cannot be used, and is really the preparation of the offering for a meal, the feast that cheats the act out of its negative significance. At that first sacrifice, the person making the offering reserves the greatest share for his own enjoyment, and from the latter sacrifice, what is useful, for the same purpose. This enjoyment is the negative power which puts an end both to the divine Being [*Wesen*] and to the singleness [*Einzelheit*]. (§718)

This kind of *Verstellungsspiel* (pretend-game) makes possible a disalienation[54] of substance and subject. In this cultic act of conspicuous consumption of the animal sacrificed, the divine essence (substance) is no longer outer, and the self (subject) "has consciousness of its unity with the divine Being." Incidentally, this is one of the instances where Hegel plays with the analogy of Greek paganism to Christianity, in order to elevate Hellenist sacral culture, as Hyppolite points out.[55] In his description of sacrificial offerings, Hegel refers—quite unmotivated—to one God, e.g., in the phrase of *Zeichen eines Gottes* ("sign of a god"), although he proceeds to mention two oppositional divine forces, namely Apollo and Dionysus; also often, when he mentions Ceres and Bacchus, he tends to allude to the Christian mysteries of bread and wine (§723).

In the abstract cult, the Greek gods to be worshipped are those who control the powers of the upper law (Apollo), "which has blood and actual life" and those who control the powers of the lower law (Ceres and Bacchus). The latter Dionysian divinities have vampire-like qualities. They "possess in bloodless form secret and cunning power" (§718). These opposing powers resurface in Hegel's discussion of tragedy: here, the upper law is associated with Phoebus, the sun god, god of daylight, (i.e., Apollo) and the lower law with the furies (Erinyes), an epithet of Ceres (§738). In these play of forces, Apollo, who as bringer of light also brings life, clearly warrants the upper hand, since Dionysus, the "god of many names," "hides" behind the masks of Ceres and Bacchus, and infuses the game with destructive power.

These divine forces are a playful *Leitfaden* throughout the chapter on "*Kunstreligion*." In the *living work of art*, the cultic worship is no longer a worship of a divine being, 'as the empty Depth" (§720) but as Spirit. The gods are no longer represented by statues but by the self-conscious people. The worshipper knows himself to be in unity with the Spirit; he recognizes his self in its Substance, i.e., "he knows himself to be at one with the divine essence."[56] But this unity is only externally realized, as corporality. It is epitomized in the athlete who represents the "inspired [*beseeltes*], living" artwork (§725). "The handsome warrior [*Fechter*] is indeed the glory of his particular nation, but he is a corporeal individuality" who lacks the spiritual essence (§726). Clearly, Apollo, who takes on the shape of the lifeless beautiful statue in the abstract artwork, now assumes the body of the beautiful athlete and torchbearer. In the living artwork,

Bacchanalian frenzy, the self's "wild stammering utterance," still dominates so that the self is "beside itself" (*außer sich*), out of sync or out of balance. The self only grasps the mysteries of Ceres and Bacchus, not—as Hegel emphasizes—those of the upper gods, who infuse the self with individuality (§724). The raptured worshipper's rationality is clouded and lacks Apollonian clarity. A true unity with the Absolute is only accomplished in the higher (spiritual) form of language of epos, tragedy, and comedy (§726).

In their realization of the form of the living artwork, the Greek *Volk* recognizes that it has to overcome hubris, embodied in the Bacchantes, a swarm of roaming, frenzied women (*schwärmende Weiber*, §723). Here, Hegel's Aristotelian streak comes out *tout de force* for trying to combat hubris; he calls for temperance by envoking the "civilizing" element of the festivals where thus unconscious, delirious exuberance (*Schwärmerei*) can be tamed and a unity of opposites be realized.

> This undisciplined revelry of the god must bring itself to rest as an *object*, and the enthusiasm which did not attain to consciousness must produce a work that confronts it, . . . but not however, as an intrinsically lifeless, but as a *living*, self. Such a Cult is the festival which man celebrates in his own honor. (§725)

Curiously, Hegel makes no mention of the necessity of an equilibrium, a balance between the Dionysian and Apollonian forces in the section of the abstract artwork, where, presumably, the untamed Bacchantes express themselves in lyric songs and oracles. However, Hegel also toys with the Dionysian attribute "god of many names" who in the shape of an earth spirit (*Erdgeist*) goes through metamorphoses of the feminine principle of nutritional, objective substance to the masculine principle of spiritual, self-conscious, subjective *Dasein*. These principles refer respectively to the powers of Ceres, goddess of agriculture, and Bacchus, god of wine. They also point to a not-so-subtle division of nature and culture, where the fruits of Ceres represent the former and the cultivated wine the latter. The determinate negation of these opposites, i.e., of pure immanence and transcendence, occurs in the spiritual work of art, in the language of epic, tragedy, and comedy.

In the section on the *spiritual artwork*, the opposites do persist in a different shape. In the *epos*, we find the extremes in the Olympian gods (*Gesamthimmel*) on the one hand and the *Gesamtvolk* on the other, whereby the bard, who narrates the story, functions as a vanishing mediator (between universality of the divine and singularity of the human). The pathos of the bard is not the immediate tranquilizing force of nature, i.e., it is not a Bacchic force, but it is a reflective, Apollonian power of recollection (Mnemosyne). The bard is simply the organ, "it is not his own self that counts but his muse, his universal song" (§729, Baille, trans.). But Hegel does not fail to stress a certain comic element vis-à-vis the role of the gods in the epic which displaces the serenity of the bard's passion. Taylor (1975) notes that the gods are parochial universals—not identical with the truly universal self [57]—so that the gods are cast as being not all too different from the heroic humans depicted in these narratives, such as the *Iliad*. Hegel remarks that "[t]he earnestness of those divine powers is a ridiculous superfluity," while at the same time the superhuman work performed by the mortal heroes is equally done in vain, since the gods toy with them cunningly and steer them into their predetermined fate (§730). Due to their own parochial nature, the gods also compete with each other, which represents "a comic self-forgetfulness of their eternal nature." In this play of the forces, of divine excess and heroic restraint, of seriousness and purposelessness, the divine actions are sheer mockery and provide comic relief. Hegel explains that "[o]ne purpose of the activity . . . is an arbitrary showing-off which at once melts away and transforms the apparent earnestness [*anscheinenden Ernst*] of the action into a harmless, self-confident play, without result or outcome" (§731). However, these contigent comic actions cannot escape the "iron dice of necessity"—to invoke a Nietzschean expression. Hegel plays with a representation of necessity by introducing a dialectical play, a free-play which unites the opposites in the form of the self-mediating Concept.

> This Necessity, however, is the *unity* of the Notion which brings under control the contradictory substantial being of the separate moments, a unity in which the inconsistency and arbitrariness of their action is orderly disposed, and *the play of its actions which retains its earnestness and worth in the actions themselves.* The content of the world of pictorial thought [*Vorstellung*] freely unfolds [*spielt los-gebunden*] itself in the *middle term* [of its own movement], gathering itself round the individuality of a hero who, however, in his strength and beauty feels his life is broken and sorrowfully awaits an early death. (§732, emphasis added)

This is one of the key passages of the PhS which lays out Hegel's thoughts about play and clarifies that play *is* the unity of the Concept. It amounts to a *play* which is serious and negates the "spirit of gravity," the self-pity, that holds sway of the tragic hero, as narrated by the bard, who remains *außer sich* (beside himself) and vanishes in his performative play. Equally, it dissolves the pompous, mocking games of the warring gods. Yet, the process of negation, of vanishing, does not entail that the self is completely dissolved into its other. To use a Lacanian term: there is an *objet petit a*, the "stuff" of the empty form (subject) which resists objectification.[58]

The Concept only becomes aware of itself in "the higher language" of *tragedy* where its power of the negative holds sway over the human and divine worlds. In tragedy, the Concept collects and unifies the polarized moments of the minstrel who becomes the actor and of the divine, abstract nonactual necessity. Both extremities which remain unmediated in the epos, Hegel explains, have to approach the content of the play: "one of them, Necessity, has to fill itself with the content, the other, the language of the Minstrel, must participate in it" (§732). Hence, mediation, determinate negation, occurs in tragedy where the minstrel's narrative is replaced by the chorus and the bard becomes the actor. Thus, the hero's anguish is not merely narrated but dramatically impersonated by an actor.

The importance of masks (*personae*) that the hero dons must be emphasized. Is the actor "other" from his mask? Is he merely hiding *behind* the disguise or is he in fact *becoming* the impersonation? Is there a standpoint beyond the masks?

In embarking on this phenomenological journey, Spirit plays with one masquerade after another but never quite seems to discard the previous mask that no longer "fits"; on the contrary, the previous disguises are exteriorized (*entäussert, entfremdet*), yet woven into the new fabric, be it self-consciousness or Reason, through Spirit's tarrying with the negative power. The mask is not accidental to the player, but an essential part. Hegel, the dialectician-trickster, never suggests to throw away a mask—instead, it can only be put on and piled up. This is Hegel's postmetaphysical gesture.

The supreme god of masks is Dionysus. Tragedy has a Dionysian character since Dionysus, in his double identity of life and death, needs the mask to symbolize this doubleness. The actor who masquerades, Otto (1933) explains somewhat mysteriously, plays with—and is enthralled by—the Dionysian force: "The actor is in awe of the eminence of those beings who are no longer present. He is himself yet is another. Rapture, frenzy have touched him, revealed something of the secret of the frenzied god, of the spirit of doubleness, which lives in the mask, whose last descendent is the actor."[59]

Dieter Bremer (1986) argues convincingly that Hegel's notion of tragedy is anti-Aristotelian and returns to a pre-Aristotelian conception of justice as presented in the trilogy of the Orestea by Aeschylus. While Hegel repeats metaphors in the chapter on "*Sittliches Recht*" from Sophocles' *Antigone*, it is Aeschylus's notion of conciliation that is the driving force in the art-religion chapter and motivates Hegel's discussion of Greek tragedy.[60] Unlike modern art theory, Hegel maintains that tragedy has a character of conciliation, is able to mediate the conflicts that arise in the play.[61] Bremer also discusses Hegel's lectures on aesthetics, in which he represents the Greek chorus as the non-dirempted consciousness of the Divine. The soothsaying, passive chorus is in opposition to tragic, conflict-ridden individuals and both find their mediation in the Greek tragedy.[62]

Hegel's emphasis on *Versöhnung* is much more pronounced in his later work in the lectures on aesthetics and philosophy of religion, than in his *Phenomenology*. Bremer tends to gloss over the import of the conflict-laden *Antigone* for Hegel's theory of tragedy.[63] Antigone's suicide is an instance of a successful self-externalization into the object, i.e., there is no *objet petit a* left over.[64] But note that successful negation "spoils" Hegel's dialectical game since it negates the Dionysian flux.

In tragic art, curiously, the chorus does not represent Bacchic women (furies); Hegel maintains that they articulate pity, are in calm repose, and thus have clearly Apollonian traits. Tragic action, on the other hand, is dirempted into Dionysian and Apollonian forces. These spiritual powers intermittently battle with the human, natural powers whose antagonism lies in the feminine and the masculine ethical poles (cf. Antigone and Creon). Apollo is under siege by the lower, subterranean-dwelling (*im Hinterhalte lauernde Macht*) Furies (Erinyes), who are associated with Demeter and Dionysus[65] (§738). Bremer notes that sublation occurs on two levels: through *lethe*,[66] forgetfulness of the heinous crime, and through the unifying spiritual power of Zeus.[67]

Tragedy fails for two reasons. First, it lacks an element of irony and misunderstands the role of masks donned for the performative act of reconciliation. Therefore it does not recognize that the heavens have become depopulated (gods have to become humans and thus irrelevant) and plays into anthropomorphism instead of mocking it (as already demanded by Heraclitus). Secondly, it does not recognize that the warring powers both err or hold morally equivalent just positions.

Whereas in tragedy, the extreme powers of Apollo and the Erinyes are unified in the ethical substance, i.e., in Zeus, now, in *comedy*, which is the final stage of art-religion, the god of masks wins out by mocking the logos, the True and Beautiful, indeed by playing tricks on what is dear to philosophical thought.[68] It turns out to be a comic spectacle, since in comedy the Platonic *kalokagathia*, the ideas of the Beautiful and the Good, are relegated to the play of opinions (§746). Hegel also echoes, as Desmond (1992) argues, the Socratic spirit of irony; Greek comedy reveals the absolute negating power of subjectivity.[69] The "death of god" is linked to Socrates and comedy, which represents the decline of the tragic age.

Hyppolite (1974) notes that whereas in tragedy the actor embodies the divine through his mask, in comedy the actor simply "jettisons his mask and appears on stage in flesh and blood."[70] However, I do not think that this is the implied meaning of the sentence about the hero who "dissolves [*zerfällt*] into his mask and . . . his actual self" (§742), which is the work of Dionysus, whose attribute is *lusios* (who breaks ties between the human and the divine). But what is this naked self, this vessel self? Is it devoid of masks? No, after all, Hegel also emphasizes the unity of the player with his *persona*—the self is conscious of his "collapse" (*Zusammenfall*): "the actual self of the actor coincides with what he impersonates [i.e., the *persona* or mask]." The spectator is also drawn into the theatrical representation, since he imagines himself in those roles and is "truly at home" by observing them (§747).

Desmond (1992) concurs with Hyppolite that in comedy there is no longer a unity of actor and mask. I also disagree with Desmond's interpretation that with the emergence of self-consciousness there is a neat separation of persona and actor.[71] Desmond holds further that "the divine mask is shown to be just that, a mask. This divine mask is a game that we cannot play naively." Surely, in the movement of spirit, the self plays with the idea of demythologizing, debunking of the gods, but, as Desmond puts it, it is unaware that the gods laugh back![72] Hence, it is puzzling to me that the self has indeed cleansed itself of any masks if it is unable to sustain the mockery by answering back. In fact, about the naive comfort that self-consciousness takes refuge in, Hegel says, "It is the return of everything universal into the certainty of itself which, in consequence, is this complete loss of fear and of essential being on the part of all that is alien. This self-certainty is a state of spiritual well-being and of repose therein, such as is not to be found anywhere outside of this Comedy"(§747).

Hegel plays with this state of comfort that consciousness takes pleasure in; it is a state of *Wohlsein und Sichwohlseinlassen*—a mocking pun, not quite captured in Miller's translation (of well-being and repose). Desmond concludes that we (the spectators?) need to wait for a new mask, namely *Geist*, which is also the ultimate disguise.[73] Clearly, Hegel imitates Aristophanes' comic demythologizing by suggesting that in comedy gods become clouds. However, he does not hold that the self becomes self-transparent to itself by tossing the masks of the divinities away. Mockery of that which is alien turns into self-mocking introspection; happy, comic consciousness learns it is in fact unhappy consciousness for it realizes that the cunning of reason has new masks waiting in the wings for the torn self, grieving over the loss of substance. This grief is expressed in the harsh saying that "God is dead" (§752).

Masks in Hegel's PhS are important tools that play alongside substance qua transcendental subjectivity, that is in the movement of *Beiherspielen.* Dionysian masks are treacherous, carrying both life-spending and death-giving energies; comic consciousness necessarily is the Janus-face of unhappy consciousness. As Desmond (1992) puts it poignantly, we bear witness to a comedy of failure, in which the unhappy consciousness signifies the split of the self and radical metaphysical failure.[74] Butler (1987) applies this idea to the general rhethoric of PhS which is such that tragic blindness turns out to be comic cartoonlike myopia.[75]

Social and Political Implications of Hegel's Play

Much of Hegel's discussion of play is written in an emphatic witty style which does not merely demonstrate that the PhS is narrated as a comedy of failure, but also suggests that it is simply telling a series of jokes, without letting us know exactly how Hegel plays his tricks. I also agree with Westphal (1979) that the PhS gives us a social history of transcendental subjectivity. In that case, we also need to investigate the political significance of this historical narrative and to uncover any ideological weaknesses. Much has been written on the ethico-political dimensions of the PhS by feminists,[76] so that I will restrict myself to a discussion of the aesthetico-political issues pertaining to the section on religion.

In the section on what Hegel dubiously calls Natural Religion, there are quite a few examples that manifest a clearly ideologically motivated discussion, reflecting his romanticist, Helleno-phile penchant: The pyramids are not works of art but merely objects (*Dinge*) produced instinctively, "as bees build their honeycomb" (§691)—which echoes Schiller's *thierischer Kreis*. These objects are works which lack consciousness. Indeed, they are "monsters in shape, word, and deed" (§698). These descriptions of so-called Natural—or primitive—Religion reveal an unreconstructed attitude of cultural imperialism, which grants only classical Greece (not Persia, Egypt, India, etc.) as true predecessor of Christian culture and the German Enlightenment a "manifest destiny" [*sic*]. One might ask what has come of the Jewish tradition? Cutrofello states that Hegel,

> [t]he absolute knower who affirmed the notional truth to revealed religion was himself an *implicit* anti-Semite, in that he . . . could recognize only those whom he viewed as having been raised to the absolute standpoint by way of revealed religion. However, . . . the absolute knower had thrown off the picture-thinking of

revealed religion, and as such he could repress the moment of his anti-Semitism.[77]

Hegel does not revise his position in his later works. In the *Philosophy of Religion* manuscript, which differentiates between the "dark" primitive religions and Greek "enlightened," i.e., spiritual, religion, Hegel compares different degrees of intuition in the form of the cultus and remarks that "it is . . . the intuition of the process, of the transition from savagery to legality, from barbarism to ethical life, from unconscious dullness to the self-illuminating certainty of self-consciousness" (*Philosophy of Religion*, Vol. I, 178). Thus is the "play of the movement" of the subjective side of the cultus. Furthermore, Hegel's romanticization of the playfulness of classical Greece is problematic. It is one of the few instances where he gives a hint of being enamored with the idea that there is something like good authentic play exemplified in Greek culture.

Besides the clearly Eurocentric bias in his aesthetic and religious writings, Hegel also emphasizes the necessity (and beauty) of gendered play worlds. He maintains that there are two ethical poles in tragedy: On the one hand there is the "feminine" sphere, pertaining to Nature, human law, subterranean forces, and the family (with such attributes as being bloodless, lifeless, dark, secretive, and endowed with cunning powers); on the other hand, there is the "masculine" sphere of importance (culture, divine law, *polis*) which displays attributes reminiscent of a (neo-)Platonic metaphysics of light: blood, life, light, revealed, transparent knowledge (cf. §736). Other opposites are those of the virile Apollo vis-à-vis the emasculated/effeminate Dionysus, the latter alternatively appears in the forms of Bacchus and Ceres (in the discussion of rites that involve sacrificial acts) and in the shape of the revenging Erinyes in the Greek tragic drama.

In the section on the living artwork Hegel comforts his feminist reader with the following observation regarding the metamorphoses of the (female) earth spirit: "Through the utility of being able to be eaten and drunk, nature attains its highest perfection; in effect in this act nature is the possibility of a higher existence and comes close to the confines of spiritual Dasein" (§721, Baille trans.). This explanation of the ascension toward transcendental subjectivity is Hegel's grand gesture towards the emancipation of women, as he perhaps realized that the political demands of the Republican women, who helped spearheading the French Revolution, were not totally baseless. However, these women only "come close" to self-actualization: Hegel does not overcome his addiction to Aristotle's theory of the complementary nature of the sexes. Apollo clearly rules in the male and civic sphere of knowledge and Dionysus or the Erinyes, in the female, private sphere of nonknowledge, i.e., intuition (cf. §739). Hegel's play is an *aesthetic* play and as such of limited political value for *hoi polloi* and subaltern subjects, since it caters towards patriarchal, bourgeois, and Eurocentric sensibilities.

However, we get a glimpse of "subversion" when Hegel dons an ironic mask in his social commentary. In a few passages on religious practices, Hegel is not only hard pressed to hold back his endorsement of Greek paganism (over Christianity) but also barely veils his anti-Catholic sentiment. In the Abstract Artwork, Hegel points out that the Greeks believed that they cleansed themselves from sinful acts simply by donning white clothes and performing sacral rites (§715). This exteriorization of the soul is also present in the practices of the papal indulgences, against which Luther raged in his 95 theses. Hegel also jokes about the "selfless" act of fancy decoration of the temple, which supposedly is a humble gesture towards some benign god, but in fact has a real use value for human consumption, i.e., the enjoyment of one's own riches (§§718-719). This is perhaps Hegel's ironic stance toward the (Catholic) baroque churches and the conspicuous consumption of the believers' gifts (i.e., taxation) by the papal power and his other beneficiaries.

In conclusion, Hegel makes an important contribution to play theory, which I have tried to show in elucidating different passages in the PhS. Particularly, in declaring the self-moving Concept as play, as a Bacchanalian revel, he has stepped outside the "logocentric" tradition. Furthermore, as Desmond (1986) points out, Hegel attempts to unite Schiller's *Form-* and *Stofftrieb* and Nietzsche's Apollonian and Dionysian elements in the artwork which Hegel determines as a concrete universal or a spiritualization of the sensuous.[78] As his discussion on tragedy indicates, Hegel seeks the unity of the interplay between knowledge and intuition (Apollo vs. Erinyes), which comes to the fore through the self-conscious, masked actor. The player is thus "subject to the cunning of reason in aesthetic form"; in other words, he is subjected to the interplay of freedom and necessity.[79] But I disagree with Desmond (1986) who denies that the history of beauty for Hegel is a narrative of subsequent failures; Desmond maintains that the unity of opposites does bring about affirmation, namely positive, speculative Reason![80] Such closure is, however, not the game of the cunning of reason. Butler (1987) has best captured the playful "spirit" of the PhS, echoed in Zizek (1993), that absolute truth is the "dramatic integrity of a comedy of errors." Hence, the PhS "is a study in fiction-making which shows the essential role of fiction and false belief in the quest for philosophical truth."[81]

Notes

1. Cf. Judith Butler, *The Subjects of Desire* (New York: Columbia University, 1987).

2. Hegel's play with contradictions comes to the fore with his description of cultic practice, which is "as serious playing and a playful seriousness, a gravity that is gay" (*Lectures on the Philosophy of Religion*, Vol. I, 168). Hegel breaks with Aristotle's postulate of differentiating between play and seriousness.

3. *Einleitung in die Geschichte der Philosophie*, 299. ("Alles Spielerische achten wir nicht als etwas Hohes, sondern als etwas gegen die Form des Gedankens tiefer Stehendes.")

4. Martin Heidegger, *Hegel's Concept of Experience* (New York: Harper and Row, 1970), 168.

5. Eugen Fink, *Hegel: Phänomenologische Interpretationen der Phänomenologie des Geistes*, Frankfurt: Klostermann, 1977a), 344.

6. Incidentally, Andrew Cutrofello's *The Owl at Dawn. A Sequel to Hegel's* Phenomenology of Spirit (Albany: SUNY, 1995) plays out this theme par excellence.

7. I.e. *beiherspielend*.

8. Cf. Fink, 1977a, 107.

9. On this point cf. McCumber, *The Company of Words: Hegel, Language, and Systematic Philosophy* (Evanston: Nortwestern University, 1993), 66, who states that Hegel's own account of truth eliminates "from its domain almost everything we would ordinarily call 'true'—things like sentences, propositions, and beliefs: Hegel is willing to admit that sentences, propositions, and beliefs are bearers, but of 'correctness,' a quality which coincides with what the correspondence theory calls 'truth'." Hegel holds that this kind of truth which only seeks "correctness" has limits, insofar as it does not question the tools (concepts, etc.) it uses for the analysis of assertions (cf. 63). Despite the limitations of the correspondence theory Hegel does not render it into abstract negation.

10. Cf. Butler, 1987, 22-23; Desmond, *Beyond Hegel and Dialectic* (New York: SUNY, 1992) chap. 5.

11. Desmond, 1992, 150.

12. Desmond, 1992, 153.

13. Desmond, 1992, 156.

14. Cf. J. N. Findlay, *Hegel's* Phenomenology of Spirit, trans., A.V. Miller (Oxford: Clarendon, 1977), xxix.

15. A sentiment echoed by Nietzsche's fascination with the mythic figure of the Hellenic noble warrior.

16. Richard Norman, *Hegel's Phenomenology: A Philosophical Introduction* (New York: St. Martin's, 1976), 122.

17. Desmond, 1992, 137.

18. Ibid., his emphasis.

19. Desmond, 1992, 138.

20. The erotic absolute is marked by lack or indeterminacy to be overcome over time. The agapeic absolute, on the other hand, is overdetermined, infinite. It cannot be mediated in the finite moment (cf. Desmond, 1992), 78-79.

21. Desmond, 1992, 80.

22. Desmond, 1992, 284.

23. As Krell put it in a different context in David Krell, "Hegel Heidegger Heraclitus," in *Heraclitean Fragments*, ed. J. Sallis and K. Maly (University of Alabama, 1980), 23.

24. Howard Williams, *Hegel, Heraclitus and Marx's Dialectic* (New York: St. Martin's, 1989), 11.

25. With respect to Heraclitus's organization of the oneness of opposite phenomena, Guerrière's "Physis, Sophia, Psyche" in *Heraclitean Fragments*, ed. J. Sallis and K. Maly (University of Alabama, 1980, 103) states a sixfold division: "The opposites are one (1) in origin, (2) in cognitive coincidence, (3) in evaluative coincidence, (4) in cyclic recurrence, (5) in evaluative correlativity, and (6) in a dialectic of metaphors". He emphasizes that the various oppositional elements are one, insofar as they "manifest the one physis operative beneath their surface."

26. Cf. Johannes Hirschberger, *Kleine Philosophiegeschichte* (Freiburg: Herder, 1983), 164.

27. Jean Hyppolite *Genesis and Structure of Hegel's* Phenomenology of Spirit, trans. S. Cherniak and J. Heckman (Evanston: Northwestern University, 1974/1946), 421.

28. Fink, 1977a, 33.

29. Fink, *Sein und Mensch: Vom Wesen der ontologischen Erfahrung* (Freiburg: Alber Verlag, 1977b), 66-67.

30. Fink, 1977a, 215-16.

31. Fink, 1977a, 172.

32. Desmond, *Art and the Absolute* (New York: SUNY, 1986), more solemnly, describes the phrase as relying on the tradition of the aesthetic theodicy, e.g., of Plato, Aquinas.

33. Hyppolite, 1974, 421.

34. I am grateful to Alison Brown for a clarification on this point. However, Robert Ackermann, *Nietzsche: A Frenzied Look* (Amherst: University of Massachusetts, 1990) takes the Dionysian to be the fundamental form of art; the Apollonian is merely representing the Dionysian in *Birth*, 15.

35. I owe this point to Marcella Tarozzi Goldsmith. Cf. also William Maker's valuable book which suggests that the PhS serves as an introduction to Hegel's systematic philosophy—as laid out in the *Science of Logic*—and as introduction, the PhS has to narrate the "road of despair," the necessary negation of absolute knowledge (William Maker, *Philosophy Without Foundations: Rethinking Hegel*, Albany: SUNY Press, 1994, cf. Chapter 3).

36. Slavoj Zizek, *Tarrying with the Negative. Kant, Hegel, and the Critique of Ideology* (Durham: Duke University, 1993), 243-44; his emphasis.

37. Zizek, 1993, 31.

38. Zizek, 1993, 166-7.

39. Zizek, 1993, 33.

40. Cf §47 "the single shapes of Spirit do not persist any more than determinate thoughts do, but they are as much positive and necessary moments, as they are negative and evanescent."

41. Cf. Walter Otto, *Dionysos, Mythos und Kultus* (Frankfurt: Klostermann, 1933).

42. Zizek, 1993, 25.

43. Zizek, 1993, 25.

44. Cf. Hans-Georg Gadamer's article "Die Stellung der Poesie im System der Hegelschen Ästhetik" (in: *Welt und Wirkung von Hegels Ästhetik, Hegel-Studien* Beiheft 27, ed. A. Gethmann-Siefert and O. Pöggeler (Bonn: Bouvier Verlag, 1986b) for a discussion of the pecularity of the term, 219-220.

45. Hyppolite, 1974, 544.

46. Hegel's discussion of 'natural' religion is rather cursory and takes up only a third of the interpretation of either Greek art-religion or Christianity. I will discuss Hegel's ideologically motivated discussion below.

47. Desmond, 1992, 319.

48. Cf. *Philosophy of Religion*, Vol.I, 170.

49. Hyppolite, 1974, 548.

50. However, this passage seems to be indicative of Hegel's mystic proclivity, in particular of his fondness of Jacob Boehme, a Protestant mystic.

51. Andrew Cutrofello, "The Blessed Gods Mourn," *The Owl of Minerva* 28(1) (1996), 34.

52. Hyppolite, 1974, 551.

53. Term borrowed from Zizek, 1993.

54. Cf. Zizek, 1993, 34.

55. Hyppolite, 1974, 552.

56. Hyppolite, 1974, 552.

57. Charles Taylor, *Hegel* (Cambridge: Cambridge University, 1975), 205.

58. Cf. Zizek, 1993, 21.

59. Otto, 1933, 190.

60. Bremer "Hegel und Aischylos" in *Welt und Wirkung von Hegels Ästhetik, Hegel-*

Studien Beiheft 27, ed. A. Gethmann-Siefert and O. Pöggeler (Bonn: Bouvier Verlag, 1986b), 231-33.

61. Bremer, 1986, 238.

62. Cf. Bremer, 1986, 226.

63. Bremer, 1986, 239.

64. Curiously, as Patricia Mills in *Woman, Nature, and Psyche* (New Haven, Conn.: Yale University, 1987) notes, Hegel never mentions her suicide in his discussion of Sophocles' play.

65. Even though Hegel focuses here on Greek tragedy, he employs the Latin names (Ceres and Bacchus) instead of using Demeter and Dionysus for the gods of Hades.

66. Bremer (1986) remarks that Hegel preempts Heidegger's discovery of *aletheia* as unforgetfullness.

67. Bremer, 1986, 232.

68. Mocking the logos of course also means taking it seriously qua logos—not relegating it into abstract negation. Irony in Hegel—not unlike mimesis in Plato—has an unstable existence; in the *Philosophy of Right* it is strongly condemned. I am grateful to Marcella Tarozzi Goldsmith for clarifying this point.

69. Desmond, 1992, 292.

70. Hyppolite, 1974, 556.

71. Cf. Desmond, 1992, 293.

72. Cf. 1992, 294.

73. Cf. 1992, 295.

74. 1992, 279-80.

75. Butler, 1987, 21.

76. In his article "The Woman in White: On the Reception of Hegel's *Antigone*," Martin Donougho (1989) critiques the feminist responses (of Mills 1986; Irigaray 1985; and Nussbaum 1986) and notes that Hegel opposed the patriarchical tendencies of the Greeks, but nevertheless he failed to note this bias in his own time, 86. Ravven (1988) is even more generous in her defense of Hegel, and claims that Hegel gives a non-prescriptive picture of the social constructed personality of woman in the PhS, Heidi Ravven, "Has Hegel Anything to Say to Feminists?" *Owl of Minerva* 19:2 (1988), 155. Cf. also P. J. Mills, ed., *Feminist Interpretations of Hegel: Re-Reading the Canon* (University Park: Penn State University, 1996) and Andrew Cutrofello's feminist construction of Hegel's *Bildungsroman* in his *The Owl at Dawn* (1995).

77. Cutrofello, 1995, 92.

78. Desmond, 1992, 22.

79. Desmond, 1986, 63.

80. Desmond, 1986, 114. In all fairness I should mention that it seems that Desmond (1992) has revised his thoughts on this and sides with Butler by stating that the PhS is a mockery of Logos.

81. Butler, 1987, 23.

Postlude

Surrealist games are an exquisite foretaste of the surrealist life that one day will be enjoyed by everybody. Against the miserabilist order, with its ever-present concentration camps, the surrealist revolution defines itself as an anarchist *festival.* Surrealism versus miserabilism also signifies *free play* versus *slave labor.*

—Franklin Rosemont, *The Only Game in Town,* 1978

Deleuze's work *Difference and Repetition* (1994) singles out Hegel and Plato as key culprits who engage in (bad) identitarian thinking and thus malign difference. Whatever falls out, be it playfulness, deception, or myths, finds itself reduced to the nonidentitarian other and is repressed. Myths in Plato, Deleuze notes, are incorporated into the true dialectical method only if they "behave"—if they don't run amok over our rational, Apollonian, sensibilities. Masqueraded selves in Hegel feign participation in Bacchanalian orgies. Behind these masks, though, lurks the god of proper representation, of truth, Apollo. No decentering, displacement takes place in this dialectical movement, Deleuze claims: "[it is] a world in which one is only apparently intoxicated, in which reason acts the drunkard and sings a Dionysian tune while nonetheless remaining 'pure' reason" (264). Feigning intoxication or madness is also a recurrent theme in Plato's dialogues. Socrates is the sole person at symposia, who either can "take it" or feigns imbibing, in order to remain sober and use his condition to coerce others—who have truly succumbed to stupor—to agree with his position.

Yet, Hegel's revel accomplishes something quite different. Deleuze conveniently disregards the destructive force of the self's tarrying with the negative, staring into the abyss of that world. Every member drawn into the revel is indeed intoxicated and not just apparently so. Undoubtedly, Deleuze's sympathies rest with Nietzschean playful spirits, and he may be troubled by life-affirming interpretations of Platonic and Hegelian myth- and mask-making. Certainly, it seems odd to advance a defense of Hegel's and Plato's Dionysian playfulness. However, Hegel recognizes that there is no doer, no essence behind the mask; thus playful performativity is not used to cover up superficially some serious underlying content. Plato, too, gives space to frenzied, nonrational expressions in his myths and allegories and in his irreverent display of Socrates as satyr in the *Symposium.*

I have argued that Aristotle rather than Plato is guilty of provoking a malediction of play so that play becomes the Other of reason in Western metaphysics. Deleuze concedes that even though Plato initiates an exocization of simulcra, it is Aristotle who enforces such malediction (265). What needs to be exorcized are "free, oceanic differences, . . . nomadic distributions and crowned anarchy" (265). I show that Aristotle functions as a "spoilsport" insofar as he breaks with the sophist cunning and attributes to play a merely instrumental value: it is good only for relaxation to improve one's work afterwards and play qua child's play has a recognizable value for moral education. But play has intrinsic worth only when it is purged from excessive, Dionysian elements, i.e., when it is contained in a purely Apollonian framework. Such purified, serious play is called *schole* (leisure) in Aristotle's ethics.

In the three chapters which outline the conception of play in the ancient Hellenic world, I have contrasted and compared the play of thinkers and poets with that of Aristotle. In the Presocratic world of play, notably in Homer and Heraclitus, playfulness is not yet cast in opposition to the concept of seriousness. Furthermore, the Dionysian and Apollonian play impulses are employed in these narratives without being maligned. The unity of opposites occurs—*par excellence*—in Heraclitus's famous fragment on child's play (fr. B52). Hesiod's fables seem to introduce a work ethic alien to the Hellenic nobles and thus emphasizing an Apollonian, rationalistic play; however, I contend that Hesiod's poetic style suggests a fondness of Dionysian cunning in the trope of Pandora, so that both elements inform his conception of play. In Euripides' tragedies the Dionysian comes to the fore again, for which he finds himself being ridiculed by Aristophanes.

In Plato we see a shift towards an ethical polarization of play. Certain kinds of play are condoned while others are cautioned against in mimetic representations of reality. However, in Plato's dialogical style we see a surfacing of Dionysian playfulness, which carries over into his use of myths and masquerades; these give us a different, less polarized conception of his play. Thus, Plato's game is in a dialectic tension between the Apollonian and Dionysian. To be sure, it is an agonistic struggle and it seems all too often that the Apollonian wins the upper hand (of the argument).

I pursue the Aristotelian thread of the malediction of play in Kant's and Schiller's discussions of the concept and function of play. In Kant, play has a self-referential telos (*an sich angenehm*). But in the first Critique play is treated as a negative activity, referring to the "mere" play of imagination. Play is neither knowledge, nor good in itself. In Schiller, the purpose and differentiation of play is more pronounced. He distinguishes between a transcendental play-drive and a material play-drive, favoring the more intellectual drive. Here he mirrors Aristotle's ontological differentiation between the theoretical and practical lives (*bios theoretikos* vs. *bios praktikos*). I hold that the Aristotelian malediction of play has left its traces even in philosophers who endorse play and put forth a play theory (e.g., Kant, Schiller, etc.) due to their (Apollonian) emphasis on subjectivism (ranking player over play).

Beginning with Hegel nonsubjectivist ludic possibilities resurface and are cast in the tradition of Heraclitus. In the trope of the Bacchanalian revel both Apollonian and Dionysian impulses are dialectically intertwined. Tragic play is thus put into the foreground again. Hegel also reconceptualizes the meaning of masks. In exploring the question of masks, we need to differentiate between the moment when they cover up something and when they are used "dialectically," i.e., when they are piled up. Therein lies the difference between Platonic and Hegelian dialectics. Furthermore, Hegel's "cunning of reason" promises a playful conflation of the ontological dichotomies (of subject-object, appearance-reality, mind-body).

In this book I have restricted myself to the phenomenological discussion of play being in opposition to seriousness. Another important dimension is the opposition of play and work, elucidated in Marx's philosophical writings (e.g., the 1844 manuscripts). He points out the meaningfulness of an inherently playful life in which one can rid oneself from alienated work. What is novel about Marx's theory is that he wants to show a way to overcome the dichotomy of leisurely play and labor.

At this point I want to raise the problem of whether we can and should conceptualize an authentic play, a play which occurs for its own sake (autotelic play). Can we relegate play into a purely aesthetic realm? Even in postmodern talk of pastiche and simulacra, such absolute, nonpolitical aestheticization is resisted. If anything, we have to "work" at confounding the aesthetic and political realm, while keeping in mind Benjamin's warning about the aestheticization of politics (viz. Leni Riefenstahl's *Triumph of the Will)*. Political play (e.g., of theatre) employs masquerade to elucidate. Play may have its own realm of truth (Gadamer), but nevertheless it can shed light on philosophical "noble" lies: it can allude to political corruption allegorically—exemplified by medieval court jesters, by Carneval's masquerade (in the Rheinland it had the function to ridicule the Prussian oppressive regime). Nietzsche's jester removes the ideological blinders of noble lies in philosophy. What consequences, if any, does this ludic turn have in philosophical discourse? Does play "succeed" in contemporary postmetaphysical philosophy?

As an example (for a possible sequel), I want to sketch a proposal of a materialist feminist play which uses the analytic tools of the Marxist tradition (Marx, Benjamin, Marcuse) and Nietzsche's emphasis on performativity. This approach would avoid casting play and work as opposites, and it would interrogate whether or not it is more plausible to advocate "Zero work," following Bob Black and a belief in the Marvelous, following the surrealists. In confronting and displacing the "warrior" mentality that is so prevalent in play discourse, one might turn to the play of the trickster or Coyote as advocated by cyborgian feminist Donna Haraway, which opens up the monolithic play domain for contestation by playful subaltern subjects. Such an approach might lead to a feminist reinterpretation of Dionysian powers and to a parodic, subversive play of the world.

Bibliography

Ackermann, Robert. (1990). *Nietzsche: A Frenzied Look*. Amherst: University of Massachusetts.

Aristophanes. (1928). "The Frogs." In *Eleven Comedies*. New York: Horace Liveright.

———. (1993). *Plays: Wasps, Clouds, Birds, Festival Time, Frogs*. K. McLeigh (trans.). London: Methuen Drama.

Aristotle. (1863). *Ethica Nicomachea*. L. Bywater (ed.). Oxford: Clarendon Press.

———. (1985). *Nikomachische Ethik*. F. Dirlmeier (trans.). Stuttgart: Reclam.

Auerbach, Erich. (1953). *Mimesis. The Representation of Reality in Western Literature*. Princeton, N.J.: Princeton University Press.

Bally, Gustav. (1966). *Vom Ursprung und von den Grenzen der Freiheit. Eine Deutung des Spiels bei Tier und Mensch*. Basel, Germany: Schwabe.

Bar-On, Bat-Ami (ed.). (1994). *Modern Engendering: Criticial Feminist Readings in Modern Western Philosophy*. Albany, N.Y.: SUNY.

Barris, Jeromy. (1990). *God and Plastic Surgery. Marx, Nietzsche, Freud and the Obvious*. New York: Autonomedia.

Bataille, George. (1986). *Eroticism: Death and Sensuality*. San Francisco: City Lights Books.

Behler, Ernst. (1978). "Nietzsche und die frühromantische Schule." *Nietzsche-Studien* (7), 59-96.

Benjamin, Walter. (1980). *Das Kunstwerk im Zeitalter seiner technischen Reproduzierbarkeit*, vol. 2 of *Gesammelte Schriften*. Frankfurt: Suhrkamp.

Bernays, Jacob. (1979). "Aristotle on the Effect of Tragedy." *Articles on Aristotle*, vol. 4. J. Barnes, M. Schofield and R. Sorabji (eds.), 154-65. New York: St. Martin's.

Bohm, W. (1927). *Schillers Briefe über die ästhetische Erziehung*. Halle.

Black, Bob. (1992). *Friendly Fire*. New York: Autonomedia.

Boal, Augusto. (1979). *Theatre of the Oppressed*. Charles A. McBride and Maria-Odilia Leal McBride (trans.). London: Pluto.

Von Brandenstein, Béla. (1947). *Der Mensch und seine Stellung im All. Philosophische Anthropologie*. Köln.

Bertolt Brecht. (1964). *Brecht on Theatre*. New York: Hill & Wang.

Bremer, Dieter. (1986). "Hegel und Aischylos." *Welt und Wirkung von Hegels Ästhetik. Hegel-Studien Beiheft* (27), A. Gethmann-Siefert and O. Pöggeler (eds.), 225-44. Bonn: Bouvier Verlag.

Brentlinger, John. (1970). *The Symposium of Plato*. Suzy Q. Groden (trans.). Amherst: University of Massachusetts Press.

Broadie, Sarah. (1991). *Ethics with Aristotle*. Oxford: Oxford University Press.

Brown, Alison Leigh. (1995). *Fear, Truth, Writing: From Paper Village to Electronic Community*. Albany, N.Y.: SUNY.

Brown, Wendy. (1994). "'Supposing Truth Were a Woman . . .': Plato's Subversion of Masculine Discourse." *Feminist Interpretations of Plato*. Nancy Tuana (ed.), 157-80. University Park: Penn State University Press.

Butler, Judith P. (1987). *The Subjects of Desire*. New York: Columbia University Press.

Buytendijk, Frederick. (1933). *Wesen und Sinn des Spiels. Das Spiel der Menschen und der Tiere als Erscheinungsform der Lebenstriebe*. Berlin: Wolff.

———. (1951). "Zur allgemeinen Psychology des Tanzes." *Essays in Psychology dedicated to David Katz*. Uppsala.

———. (1959). "Das Spielerische und der Spieler." In: *Das Spiel (Kongressbericht)*, 13-29.

———. (1958). "Der Spieler." *Das Menschliche*. Stuttgart.

Caillois, Roger. (1950). *L'Homme et le sacré*. Paris: Gallimard.

———. (1958). *Les jeux et les hommes. Le masque et le vertige*. Paris: Gallimard.

———. (1961). *Man, Play and Games*. New York: Free Press.

Carse, James P. (1986). *Finite and Infinite Games: A Vision of Life as Play and Possibility*. New York: Free Press.

Crawford, Donald. (1974). *Kant's Aesthetic Theory*. Madison: University of Wisconsin Press.

Curran, Angela. (1998). "Feminism and the Narrative Structures of the *Poetics*." In: *Feminist Interpretations of Aristotle*. Cynthia Freeland (ed.). University Park: Penn State University Press.

Cutrofello, Andrew. (1994). *Discipline and Critique. Kant, Poststructuralism, and the Problem of Resistance*. Albany, N.Y.: SUNY.

———. (1995). *The Owl at Dawn: A Sequel to Hegel's Phenomenology of Spirit*. Albany, N.Y.: SUNY.

———. (1996). "The Blessed Gods Mourn." In *The Owl of Minerva* 28(1), 25-38.

Dalfen, Joachim. (1974). *Polis und Poiesis: Die Auseinandersetzung mit der Dichtung bei Platon und seinen Zeitgenossen*. München: Wilhelm Fink Verlag.

Deleuze, Gilles. (1983). *Nietzsche and Philosophy*. H. Tomlinson (trans.). New York: Columbia University Press.

———. (1994). *Difference and Repetition*. New York: Columbia University Press.

Derrida, Jacques. (1981). *Dissemination*. Barbara Johnson (trans.). Chicago: University of Chicago Press.

———. (1982). *Margins of Philosophy*. Alan Bass (trans.). Chicago: University of Chicago Press.

———. (1992). *Glas: Que reste-il savoir absolu?* Paris: Denoel Gauthier.

Desmond, William. (1992). *Beyond Hegel and Dialectic*. Albany, N.Y.: SUNY

———. (1986). *Art and the Absolute*. Albany, N.Y.: SUNY

Diamond, Elin. (1989). "Mimesis, Mimicry, and the "True-Real." *Modern Drama* (32), 58-72.

Diels, H. and W. Kranz (eds.). (1987). *Die Fragmente der Vorsokratiker* (Greek and German). Stuttgart: Reclam.

Djuric, M. (1985). *Nietzsche und die Metaphysik*. Berlin.

Döring, K. and Kullmann. (eds.). (1973). *Studia Platonica. Festschrift für Hermann Gundert*. Amsterdam.

Donougho, Martin. (1989). "The Woman in White: On the Reception of Hegel's *Antigone*." In *The Owl of Minerva* 21 (1): 65-89.

Duncan, Margaret Carlisle. (1988). "Play Discourse and the Rhetorical Turn: A Semiological Analysis of *Homo Ludens*." *Play and Culture* (1), 28-42.

Ehrmann, Jaques. (1968). "Homo Ludens Revisited." *Yale French Studies* (41), 31-57.

Eigen, M. and R. Winkler. (1975). *Das Spiel: Naturgesetze steuern den Zufall*. München.

Elias, Julius. (1984). *Plato's Defense of Poetry*. Albany, N.Y.: SUNY.

Euripides. (1990). *The Bacchae*. C.K. Williams (trans.). New York: Farrar Straus & Giroux.

Eze, Emmanuel C. (ed). (1997). *Race and the Enlightenment. A Reader*. Malden, Mass.: Blackwell.

———. (2001). *Achieving Our Humanity. The Idea of the Postracial Future*. New York: Routledge.

Findlay, J. N. (ed.). (1977). *Hegel's Phenomenology of Spirit*. A.V. Miller (trans.). Oxford: Clarendon Press.

Fink, Eugen. (1977a). *Hegel: Phänomenologische Interpretationen der Phänomenologie des Geistes*. Frankfurt: Klostermann.

———. (1977b). *Sein und Mensch: Vom Wesen der ontologischen Erfahrung*. Freiburg: Alber Verlag.

———. (1960). *Spiel als Weltsymbol*. Stuttgart: Kohlhammer.

———. (1957). *Oase des Glücks: Gedanken zu einer Ontologie des Spiels*. Freiburg: Alber Verlag.

Flay, Joseph C. (1989). "Hegel, Derrida and Bataille's Laughter." In *Hegel and His Critics: Philosophy in the Aftermath of Hegel*. W. Desmond (ed.), 163-78. Albany, N.Y.: SUNY.

Foucault, Michel. (1980). *Power/Knowledge*. Colin Gordon (ed.). New York: Random House.

Fränkel, Hermann. (1960). *Wege und Formen frühgriechischen Denkens*. München.

————. (1975). *Early Greek Poetry and Philosophy*. M. Hadas and J. Willis (trans.). New York: Harcourt Brace Jovanovich.

Frazier, R. M. (ed.). (1983). *The Poems of Hesiod*, translated with introduction and comments. Norman: University of Oklahoma Press.

Friedländer, Paul. (1954). *Platon: Seinswahrheit und Lebenswirklichkeit*. Berlin: de Gruyter.

Frutinger, P. (1930). *Les Mythes de Platon.* Paris: Alcan.

Gadamer, Hans G. (1965/1986a). *Wahrheit und Methode*, vol.1 *Gesammelte Werke*, 5th ed.. Tübingen: Mohr.

————. (1986b). "Die Stellung der Poesie im System der Hegelschen Ästhetik." *Welt und Wirkung von Hegels Ästhetik, Hegel-Studien Beiheft* (27). A. Gethmann-Siefert and O. Pöggeler (eds.), 212-23. Bonn: Bouvier Verlag.

————. (1977). *Die Aktualität des Schönen: Kunst als Spiel, Symbol, und Fest*. Stuttgart.

————. (1961). "Spiel als Weltsymbol." In *Philosophische Rundschau* (9).

Gehlen, Arnold. (1962). *Der Mensch. Seine Natur und seine Stellung in der Welt*. 7th ed., Berlin.

Gigon, Olof. (1985). "Die Eudaimonia im ersten Buche der Nikomachischen Ethik." In *Aristoteles. Werk und Wirkung. Aristoteles und seine Schule*, vol. 1. J. Wiesner (ed.), 339-65. Berlin.

Gilman, Sander L. (1976). *Nietzschean Parody*. Bonn: Bouvier.

Girard, René. (1972). *La violence et le sacré*. Paris.

Griswold, Charles. (1986). *Self-Knowledge in Plato's Phaedrus*. New Haven, Conn.: Yale University Press.

Groos, Karl. (1899). *Die Spiele des Menschen*. Jena.

————. (1896). *Die Spiele der Thiere*. Jena.

Grube, G. M. A. (1974). *Plato's Republic*. Indianapolis: Hackett.

Guerrière, Daniel. (1980). "Physis, Sophia, Psyche." *Heraclitean Fragments*. J. Sallis and K. Maly (eds.), 86-134. University of Alabama Press.

Gundert, Hermann. (1965). "Zum Spiel bei Platon." *Beispiele. Festschrift für E. Fink zum 60. Geburtstag*, 188-221.

————. (1968). "Zum philosophischen Exkurs im 7. Brief." *Idee und Zahl*. H.-G. Gadamer and W. Schadewaldt (eds.), 85-105. Heidelberg.

Habermas, Jürgen. (1987). *The Philosophical Discourse of Modernity*. Boston: MIT Press.

Haigis, E. (1941). *Das Spiel als Begegnung*. Leipzig: Barth.

Halperin, David. (1990). "Why is Diotima a Woman? Platonic *Eros* and the Figuration of Gender." *Before Sexuality: The Construction of Erotic Experience in the Ancient Greek World*. D. Halperin et al. (eds.), 257-308. Princeton, N.J.: Princeton University Press.

Hans, James S. (1981). *The Play of the World*. Amherst: University of Massachusetts Press.

Hartmann, Nicolai. (1965). *Zur Grundlegung der Ontologie*. Berlin.

————. (1953). *Zur Grundlegung der Ästhetik*. Berlin.

Havelock, Eric. (1963). *Preface to Plato*. Oxford.

Hegel, G. W. F. (1986). *Phänomenologie des Geistes*, vol. 3 of *Werke*. E. Moldenhauer and K. Michel (eds.). Frankfurt: Suhrkamp.

———. (1965). *The Philosophy of Right*. T. M. Knox (trans.). Oxford: Clarendon Press.

———. (1956). *The Philosophy of History*. New York: Dover.

———. (1968). *Einleitung in die Geschichte der Philosophie. Vorlesungen 1829/30*, vol. 28 of *Werke*.

———. (1892). *Lectures on the History of Philosophy*, vol. 1. E. S. Haldane and F. H. Simpson (trans.). London: Routledge.

———. (1966). *Vorlesungen über die Philosophie der Religion*. Hamburg: Felix Meiner Verlag.

———. (1987). *Lectures on the Philosophy of Religion*, vol. 2, R. F. Brown, P. C. Hodgson, et al. (trans.). Berkeley: University of California Press.

Heidegger, Martin. (1970). *Hegel's Concept of Experience*. New York: Harper and Row.

———. (1962). *Being and Time*. J. Macquarrie and E. Robinson (trans.). New York: Harper and Rowe.

———. (1961). *Nietzsche*, vol. 1 and 2. Pfullingen: Neske.

———. (1954). *Vorträge und Aufsätze*. Pfullingen: Neske.

———. (1950). *Holzwege* (6th ed.). Frankfurt: Klostermann.

———. (1957). *Identität und Differenz*. Pfullingen: Neske.

Heidegger, Martin and Eugen Fink (1970). *Heraklit, Seminar Wintersemester 1966/67*. Frankfurt: Klostermann.

Heidemann, Ingeborg. (1968). *Der Begriff des Spiels und das ästhetische Weltbild in der Philosophie der Gegenwart*. Berlin: Gruyter.

———. (1961-1962). "Nietzsches Kritik der Metaphysik." *Kantstudien* (53), 507-43.

Hein, Hilde. (1968). "Play as an Aesthetic Concept." *The Journal of Aesthetics and Art Criticism* (27), 67-71.

Henrich, Dieter. (1992). *Aesthetic Judgment and the Moral Image of the World*. Stanford: Stanford University Press.

———. (1982). "Beauty and Freedom: Schiller's Struggle with Kant's Aesthetics." *Essays in Kant's Aesthetics*. Ted Cohen and Paul Guyer (eds.), 237-357. Chicago: University of Chicago Press.

Heraklit. (1987). "Herakleitos-Heraklit." In *Die Fragmente der Vorsokratiker*. H. Diels and W. Kranz (eds.). Stuttgart: Reclam.

Hesiod. (1983). "Works and Days." In *The Poems of Hesiod*. R. M. Frazier (ed.). translated with introduction and comments. Norman: University of Oklahoma Press.

———. (1983). "Theogony." In *The Poems of Hesiod*. R. M. Frazier (ed.). translated with introduction and comments. Norman: University of Oklahoma Press.

Hinman, Lawrence M. (1974). "Nietzsche's Philosophy of Play." In *Philosophy Today* (18), 106-24.

———. (1978). "Marx's Theory of Play," in *Philosophy and Social Criticism* (5), 191-228.

Hirschberger, Johannes. (1983). *Kleine Philosophiegeschichte*. Freiburg: Herder.

Hobbes, Thomas. (1968). *Leviathan*. New York: Penguin.

Homer. (1925). *The Iliad* (in Greek). New York: Putnam.

———. (1957). *The Iliad*. A. T. Murray (trans.). Cambridge: Harvard University Press.

———. (1990). *The Iliad*. R. Fagles and B. Knox (trans.). New York: Viking.

———. (1975). *Ilias*. W. Schadewaldt (trans.). Frankfurt: Insel.

———. (1957). *Die Odyssee*. W. Schadewaldt (trans.). Frankfurt: Insel.

———. (1996). *The Odyssey*. R. Fagles (trans.). New York: Viking.

Homiak, Marcia. (1996). "Feminism and Aristotle's Rational Ideal." In *Feminism and Ancient Philosophy*, Julia Ward (ed.), 118-37. New York: Routledge.

Huizinga, Johan. (1950). *Homo Ludens*. Boston: Beacon.

Hyppolite, Jean. (1974/1946). *Genesis and Structure of Hegel's Phenomenology of Spirit*. S. Cherniak and J. Heckman (trans.). Evanston, Ill.,: Northwestern University Press.

Irigaray, Luce. (1994). "Sorcerer Love: A Reading of Plato's *Symposium*, Diotima's Speech." Eleanor H. Kuykendall (trans.). *Feminist Interpretations of Plato*. Nancy Tuana (ed.), 181-95. University Park: Penn State University Press.

———. (1974/1985). *Speculum of the Other Woman*. Ithaca, N.Y.: Cornell University.

Jowett, Benjamin. (1964). *The Dialogues of Plato*, 4 vols. London: Oxford University.

Jünger, F. G. (1953). *Die Spiele. Ein Schlüssel zu ihrer Bedeutung*. Frankfurt.

Kahn, Charles. (1979). *The Art and Thought of Heraclitus*. Cambridge.

Kant, Immanuel. (1977). "Beobachtungen über das Gefühl des Schönen und Erhabenen." In *Vorkritische Schriften bis 1768*, vol. 2 of *Werke*. W. Weischedel (ed.). Frankfurt.

———. (1974) *Anthropology From a Pragmatic Point of View*. Mary Gregor (trans.). The Hague: Martinus Nijhoff.

———. (1983). *Anthropologie in pragmatischer Hinsicht*. W. Becker (ed.). Stuttgart.

———. (1986). *Kritik der Urteilskraft*. G. Lehmann (ed.). Stuttgart.

———.(1952). *The Critique of Judgment*. J. C. Meredith (trans.). Oxford: The Clarendon Press.

———. (1965). *The Critique of Pure Reason*. Kemp-Smith (trans.). New York: St. Martin's.

———. (1993). *Prolegomena zu einer jeden künftigen Metaphysik, die als Wissenschaft wird auftreten können*. K. Vorländer (ed.). Hamburg : Felix Meiner.

Kemal, Salim. (1992). *Kant's Aesthetic Theory*. New York: St. Martin's Press.

von Kirchmann, J.H. (1882). *Erläuterungen zu Kant's Kritik der Urtheilskraft*. Leipzig.

Klaus, G. (1968). *Spieltheorie in philosophischer Sicht*. Berlin.

Klossowski, Pierre. (1969). *Nietzsche et le cercle vicieux*. Paris: Mercure.

Kneller, Jane. (1994). "Kant's Immature Imagination." In *Modern Engendering*, Bat-Ami Bar On (ed.). Albany: SUNY.

Kowatzki, I. (1972). *Der Begriff des Spiels als ästhetisches Phänomen. Von Schiller bis Benn*. Bern.

Krell, David F. (1980). "Hegel Heidegger Heraclitus." *Heraclitean Fragments*. J. Sallis and K. Maly (eds.), 22-42. University of Alabama Press.

———. (1972). "Towards an Ontology of Play: E. Fink's Notion of Spiel." *Research and Phenomenology*, 2.

Kristeva, Julia. (1982). *Powers of Horror: An Essay on Abjection*. New York: Columbia University Press.

Kutzner, Heinrich. (1973). *Erfahrung und Begriff des Spieles: Versuch, den Menschen als spielendes Wesen zu denken*. Berlin: Bouvier.

Lamberton, Robert. (1988). *Hesiod*. New Haven, Conn.: Yale University Press.

Lazarus, Moritz. (1883). *Über die Reize des Spiels*. Berlin.

Lecercle, J. J. (1985). *Philosophy in the Looking Glass*. London.

Leigh, J. E. (1972). "Deleuze, Nietzsche and the Eternal Return." *Philosophy Today* (22) 206-23.

Levin, Susan. (1996). "Woman's Nature and Role in the Ideal *Polis*: *Republic* V Revisited." In *Feminism and Ancient Philosophy*. Julia Ward (ed.), 13-30. New York: Routledge.

Lissarrague, Francois. (1990). "The Sexual Life of Satyrs." In *Before Sexuality: The Construction of Erotic Experience in the Ancient Greek World*, D. Halperin et al. (eds.), 53-81. Princeton, N.J.: Princeton University Press.

Lugones, María. (1987). "Playfulness, 'World'-travelling, and Loving Perception." *Hypatia*, 2(2): 3-19.

Lukács, Georg. (1965). *The Historical Novel*, New York: Humanities Press.

Lutz, H. (1928). *Schillers Anschauungen von Kultur und Natur*. Berlin.

MacCary, W. Thomas. (1982). *Childlike Achilles. Ontogeny and Phylogeny in the Iliad*. New York: Columbia University.

Maker, William. (1994). *Philosophy Without Foundations: Rethinking Hegel*. Albany, N.Y.: SUNY.

Makkreel, Rudolf. (1990). *Imagination and Interpretation in Kant: The Hermeneutical Import of the Critique of Judgment*. Chicago: University of Chicago Press.

Marcuse, Herbert. (1978). *The Aesthetic Dimension: Toward a Critique of Marxist Aesthetics*. Boston: Beacon.

Marten, Rainer. (1993). *Lebenskunst*. München: Wilhelm Fink Verlag.

———. (1989). *Denkkunst: Kritik der Ontologie*. Paderborn: Schöningh.

———. (1988). *Der menschliche Mensch: Abschied vom utopischen Denken*. Paderborn: Schöningh.

Marx, Karl. (1964). *Economic and Philosophic Manuscripts of 1844*. D. Struik (ed.). M. Milligan (trans.). New York: International Publishers

Matthews, Gareth B. (1994). *The Philosophy of Childhood*. Cambridge, Mass.: Harvard University Press.

————. (1984). *Dialogues with Children*. Cambridge, Mass.: Harvard University Press.

————. (1980). *Philosophy of the Young Child*. Cambridge, Mass.: Harvard University Press.

————. (1996). "Vom Nutzen der Perplexität: Denken lehren mithilfe der Philosophie." *Rostock Philosophische Schriften*.

————. (1991). "Piaget und die Kinderphilosophie." *Zeitschrift für Didaktik der Philosophie* (1), 4-8.

————. "The Uses of Perplexity: Teaching Thinking Through Philosophy" Unpublished ms.

McCumber, John. (1993). *The Company of Words. Hegel, Language, and Systematic Philosophy*. Evanston, Ill.: Northwestern University Press.

————. (1988). "Aristotelian Catharsis and the Purgation of Woman." In *Diacritics* (Winter), 53-67.

McKeon, R. (ed.). (1941). *Basic Works of Aristotle*. New York: Random House.

Menzer, P. (1952). *Kants Ästhetik in ihrer Entwicklung*. Berlin.

Miller, A.V. (1969). *Hegel's Science of Logic*. London: Allen & Unwin.

Miller, David L. (1970). *Gods and Games: Towards a Theology of Play*. New York.

Mills, Patricia J. (ed.). (1996). *Feminist Interpretations of G.W.F. Hegel*. University Park: Penn State University Press.

————. (1986). "Hegel's *Antigone*." In: *The Owl of Minerva* (17)2: 131-52.

————. (1987). *Woman, Nature, and Psyche*. New Haven, Conn.: Yale University Press.

Nagel, Mechthild. (1998). "Play in Culture and the Jargon of Primordiality: A Critique of Huizinga's *Homo Ludens*." In *Play and Culture Studies*, vol. 1, M. C. Duncan, G. Chick, and A. Aycock (eds.). Greenwich, Conn.: Ablex Publications.

————. (2001). "Thrownness, Playing-in-the-world and the Question of Authenticity" in *Feminist Interpretations of Heidegger*, P. Huntington and N. Holland (eds.). University Park: Penn State University Press.

————. "Mothers and Monsters." Unpublished ms.

Nietzsche, Friedrich. (1962). *Philosophy in the Tragic Age of the Greeks*. M. Cowan (trans.). Chicago: Regnery.

————. (1968). *The Birth of Tragedy*. In *Basic Writings*. W. Kaufmann, (ed.). New York.

————. (1967-78). *Werke: Kritische Gesamtausgabe*, 8 vols. G. Colli and M. Montinari (eds.). Berlin.

Norman, Richard. (1976). *Hegel's Phenomenology: A Philosophical Introduction*. New York: St. Martin's.

Nussbaum, Martha C. (1986). *The Fragility of Goodness: Luck and Ethics in Greek Tragedy and Philosophy*. Cambridge.

Nye, Andrea. (1994). "Irigaray and Diotima at Plato's Symposium." In *Feminist Interpretations of Plato*. Nancy Tuana (ed.), 197-215. University Park: Penn State University Press.

Ortega, Alfonso. (1968). "Juego y verdad entre los Griegos." In *Helmantica* (19), 5-30.

Otto, Walter F. (1933). *Dionysos, Mythos und Kultus*. Frankfurt: Klostermann.

Petzelt, Alfred. (1959). "Spiel und Persönlichkcit." In *Das Spiel* (*Kongressbericht* 1959), 62-75.

Pfeffer, Rose. (1972). *Nietzsche: Disciple of Dionysus*. Lewisburg, Pa.: Bucknell University Press.

Piaget, Jean. (1951). *Play, Dreams and Imitation in Childhood*. New York: Norton.

———. (1932). *The Moral Judgment of the Child*. London: Kegan.

———. (1954). *The Construction of Reality in the Child*. New York: Basic Books.

Picart, Caroline. (1999). *Resentiment and the "Feminine" in Nietzsche's Politico-Aesthetics*. University Park: Penn State University Press.

Pieper, Josef. (1952). *Leisure. The Basis of Culture*. Alexander Dru (trans.). New York: Pantheon.

Platon. (1959). *Sämtliche Werke*. 6 vols. E. Grassi (ed.). F. Schleiermacher (trans.). Hamburg: Rowohlt.

Plato. (1995). *Phaedrus*. Nehemas and Woodruff (trans.). Indianapolis: Hackett.

———. (1964). *Laws*. Jowett (trans.). London: Oxford University Press

———. (1964). *Euthydemus*. R. K. Sprague (trans.). Indianapolis: Hackett.

Plessner, Helmuth. (1967). "Der Mensch im Spiel." In *Das Spiel: Wirklichkeit und Methode*. Werner Marx (ed.). *Freiburger Dies Universitatis*, 7-11.

———. (1961). *Lachen und Weinen: Eine Untersuchung nach den Grenzen menschlichen Verhaltens*. Bern.

———. (1982). *Mit anderen Augen: Aspekte einer philosophischen Anthropologie*. Stuttgart.

Pucci, Pietro. (1987). *Odysseus Polutropos. Intertextual Readings in the Odyssee and the Iliad*. Ithaca, N.Y.: Cornell University Press.

———. (1977). *Hesiod and the Language of Poetry*, Baltimore, Md.: Johns Hopkins University Press.

———. (1980). *The Violence of Pity in Euripides' Medea*. Ithaca, N.Y.: Cornell University Press.

Rabinow, Paul (ed.). (1984). *The Foucault Reader*. New York: Pantheon Books.

Rahner, Hugo. (1948). *Der spielende Mensch*. Einsiedeln.

Ravven, Heidi. (1988). "Has Hegel Anything to Say to Feminists?" *The Owl of Minerva* (19), 149-168.

Rilke, Rainer Maria. (1987). *Duineser Elegien*, vol.1 of *Werke*. Frankfurt: Insel.

Rorty, Amélie Oksenberg. (1980). "The Place of Contemplation in Aristotle's Nichomachian Ethics." In *Essays on Aristotle's Ethics*. Rorty (ed.). Berkeley: University of California Press.

Rüssel, Arnulf. (1953). *Das Kinderspiel*. München.

Ryle, Gilbert. (1966). *Plato's Progress*. Cambridge: Cambridge University Press.

Sallis, John. (1962). "Nietzsche's Homecoming." *Man & World* (2), 108-16.

Scheuerl, H. (1954). *Das Spiel. Untersuchungen über sein Wesen, seine pädagogischen Möglichkeiten und seine Grenzen.*

Schiller, Friedrich. (1962). "Über Anmut und Würde." In *Werke, Nationalausgabe,* vol. 20. Weimar.

———. (1962). "Über die ästhetische Erziehung des Menschen in einer Reihe von Briefen." In *Werke, Nationalausgabe,* vol. 20. Weimar.

———. (1962). "Über den Grund des Vergnügens an tragischen Gegenständen." In *Werke, Nationalausgabe,* vol. 20. Weimar.

———. (1984). *Über Kunst und Wirklichkeit. Schriften und Briefe zur Ästhetik.* C. Träger (ed.). Leipzig.

———. (1967). *On the Aesthetic Education of Man, in a Series of Letters.* E. Wilkinson and L. A. Willoughby (eds.). Oxford.

Schlick, Moritz. (1927). *Vom Sinn des Lebens.* Berlin.

Schmidt, R. (1924). "Kants Lehre von der Einbildungskraft mit besonderer Rücksicht auf die Kritik der Urteilskraft." *Annalen der Philosophie und philosophischen Kritik* (4), 1-14.

Schmidt, W. (1950). "Spiele, Feste, Festspiele." *Mythe, Mensch und Umwelt.* A. Jensen (ed.), 11-23. Bamberg.

Sdun, Winfried. (1966). "Zum Begriff des Spiels bei Kant und Schiller." In *Kantstudien* (57), 500-518.

Seerveld, C. (1978). "Early Kant and a Rococo Spirit: Setting for the Critique of Judgment." *Philosophical Reform* (43), 145-167.

Sloterdijk, Peter. (1983). *Kritik der zynischen Vernunft.* Frankfurt: Suhrkamp.

Soyinka, Wole. (1975). *The Bacchae of Euripides: A Communion Rite.* New York: Norton.

Spariosu, Mihai. (1991). *God of Many Names: Play, Poetry, and Power in Hellenic Thought from Homer to Aristotle.* Durham, N.C.: Duke University Press.

———. (1989). *Dionysus Reborn: Play and the Aesthetic Dimension in Modern Philosophical and Scientific Discourse.* Ithaca, N.Y.: Cornell University Press.

Sparshott, Francis. (1994). *Taking Life Seriously: A Study of the Argument of the Nicomachean Ethics.* Toronto: University of Toronto Press.

Spelman, Elizabeth V. (1988). *Inessential Woman.* Boston: Beacon.

Stewart, J. A. (1905). *The Myths of Plato.* New York: MacMillan.

Suits, Bernard. (1970). *The Grasshopper: Games, Life and Utopia.* Toronto. University of Toronto Press.

Taylor, Charles. (1975). *Hegel.* Cambridge: Cambridge University Press.

Trebels, Andreas Heinrich. (1967). *Einbildungskraft und Spiel: Untersuchungen zur Kantischen Ästhetik. Kantstudien-Ergänzungshefte,* 93. Bonn: Bouvier.

Vaihinger, Hans. (1927). *Die Philosophie des Als Ob. System der theoretischen, praktischen und religiösen Fiktionen der Menschheit auf Grund eines idealistischen Positivismus.* Leipzig.

Volkswein, Karin. (1991). "Play as a Path for Liberation: A Marcusean Perspective." *Play & Culture* 4 (4), 359-70.

von der Mühll, P. (ed.). (1984). *Odyssea.* Stuttgart: Teubner Verlag.

Warnke, Gloria. (1987). *Gadamer. Hermeneutics, Tradition and Reason.* Stanford: Stanford University Press.

Westphal, Merold. (1979). *History and Truth in Hegel's Phenomenology.* Atlantic Highlands, N.J.: Humanities Press.

Williams, Howard. (1989). *Hegel, Heraclitus and Marx's Dialectic.* New York: St. Martin's.

Williams, Robert J. (1988). "Play and the Concept of Farce." In *Philosophy and Literature* (12) 58-68.

Wittgenstein, Ludwig. (1953). *Philosophical Investigations.* G. E. M. Anscombe (trans.). New York: Macmillan.

———. (1975). *The Blue and Brown Books.* Oxford: Blackwell.

Wohlfart, Günter. (1991). *Also sprach Herakleitos.* Freiburg: Alber.

Wolff, Robert Paul. (1963). *Kant's Theory of Mental Activity.* Cambridge: Harvard University Press.

Zeitlin, Froma I. (1985). "Playing the Other." In *Representations II*, 63-94.

Zizek, Slavoj. (1989). *The Sublime Object of Ideology.* New York: Verso.

———. (1993). *Tarrying with the Negative. Kant, Hegel, and the Critique of Ideology.* Durham, N.C.: Duke University Press.

Index

abject, 1, 74
abstract play, 67, 69
Ackermann, R., 5, 26, 104
aesthetic play, 73, 74, 101
aesthetic pleasure, 64, 69
aesthetic theory, 3, 63, 64
aesthetics, 2
agon, 7, 9, 37, 41, 45
ananke. See necessity
anapausis, 51, 52
Anthropology from a Pragmatic Point of View, 60, 78
Apollo, 9, 10, 18, 20, 22, 77, 85, 88, 89, 91, 95, 98, 99, 101, 102, 107; god of warfare, 9
Aristophanes, 3, 8, 21, 22, 23, 56, 100, 108
Aristotle, 1, 2, 3, 4, 8, 14, 21, 23, 42, 43, 44, 47, 48, 49, 50, 51, 52, 53, 54, 55, 56, 57, 58, 59, 60, 63, 65, 71, 74, 75, 76, 78, 101, 102, 108
artist metaphysicians, 4, 81, 89
art-religion, 84, 92, 93, 98, 99, 104
Auerbach, E., 10, 11, 12, 14, 24

The Bacchae, 21, 22, 23, 24, 27, 84, 89, 91, 92
Bacchanalian revel, 34, 42, 81, 82, 83, 84, 85, 87, 88, 102, 109
Bacchic frenzy, 52, 55, 67
Begriff, 59, 69, 76, 83, 89
beiherspielen, 23, 77, 81, 93, 100
Beispiele, 3, 8, 44, 77
Benjamin, W., 57, 109

bios praktikos, 51, 108
bios theoretikos, 48, 49, 51, 108
Birth of Tragedy, 2, 3, 22, 26, 44, 56, 82, 88, 94
Black, B., 109
Boal, A., 55, 58
Brecht, B., 44
Bremer, D., 98, 105
Brentlinger, J., 3, 25, 34, 45, 77
Brown, W., 33, 37, 40, 45, 46,
Butler, J., 8, 81, 100, 102, 103, 105

chance-play, 2, 16, 20, 66
child's play, 2, 3, 7, 9, 10, 19, 20, 21, 29, 48, 51, 57, 63, 108
children, 1, 3, 4, 9, 11, 18, 19, 20, 24, 26, 49, 51, 52, 53, 57, 58, 63
Christianity, 19, 93, 95, 102, 104
comedy, 1, 26, 27, 39, 44, 53, 83, 84, 92, 93, 96, 99, 100, 102
correspondence theory of truth, 83, 88
Crawford, D., 63, 77
The Critique of Judgment, 63, 75, 77
The Critique of Practical Reason, 62, 63
The Critique of Pure Reason, 61, 63, 64, 75
crooked logos, 14, 16
cultural imperialism, 100
cultus, 83, 94, 101
cunning of reason, 89, 90, 100, 102, 109
Curran, A., 58

About the Author

Mechthild Nagel teaches social philosophy at SUNY Cortland and is coeditor of *Race, Class, and Community Identity* (2000).